ALREADY BROKEN

Mending my brokenness in pursuance of finding

My Purpose

VERN HAMIL

Published by Victorious You Press™

Charlotte NC, USA

TITLE: ALREADY BROKEN
First Printed: 2022

Cover Designer: NADIA MONSANO

ISBN: 978-1-952756-83-2

Printed in the United States of America

For details email joan@victoriousyoupress.com
or visit us at www.victoriousyoupress.com

Contents

Introduction

This story captivates my life from a young child to adulthood. It is set on the beautiful island of Jamaica, where I grew up.

As a young child, I had a medical condition that was not diagnosed; therefore, it was hard to get treatment, and even if there were treatments then, they were not affordable. While coping with this form of disability and trying to find me and love myself for who I was, the worst happened. I was raped.

I was forced into a real dilemma; I could choose to put this ugly episode behind me, or I could continue to work on controlling my medical conditions. I choose the latter.

My emotional pains eroded me, and I went into a downward spiral—where I totally lost all direction of myself. *But for the grace of God,* my spirituality was my anchor.

Writing this book took me back to my past. And in reviewing my life, I realized it was not all bad. However, I was unable to focus on the opportunities that came my way due to buried trauma. In my search to discover my purpose, I realized that unless you say "Yes!" to purpose, your life will not be fulfilled.

I have written these painful chapters to say to you, my readers, "No matter what your situation is, you too can overcome." I want to motivate you into action and inspire you to greatness.

CHAPTER ONE

The formative years

I stood in the middle of a circle surrounded by my school peers, who crowded up the schoolyard. Someone reached out and pulled on my long, braided, black hair. "Shaky, Shaky," they chanted. Another peer reached out and pulled on my accordion-pleated uniform skirt. My mom, who resided in London, had sent me the uniform. I was the only one at my school with that type of skirt, and as they pulled on the skirt—the pleats stayed intact. "Shaky," they kept chanting. And the more they taunted me, the more I would literally shake. I was at their mercy. Hot, burning tears mixed with mucus streaked down my face while they teased and laughed at me. When I started crying, they would then shout, "Cry, crybaby." Even "Crybaby" would have been better, but "Shaky" was the name they gave me. To this day, I hate that nickname.

It was on a bright summer day in August in the beautiful Parish of St. Mary when God blessed my mother with two bundles of joy. I was the firstborn of twins. My brother was perfectly healthy, yet I had this neurological disorder. At the time, medical technology was not as advanced, and even if it was, my mother would not have had the financial resources to get the help I needed. However, she spent what little she had trying to get a diagnosis. When it was time to start attending school, she realized that a diagnosis was not forthcoming.

My pre-K years were fun. My first best friend, Alva D, was like my brother, and he constantly guarded me from bullies. He was my protector. It wasn't until I got into primary school that it became challenging. In my class of twenty, I excelled in reading; however, I struggled to write. I could not hold the pen to form the letters in the script, and I was always the last one to submit my work to the teacher. When we had to write an essay, I was left out in the cold. Until one day, a classmate offered me a deal: she would write for me but only if I paid her. I said, "Yes," and I gave her my lunch money as payment. In retrospect, I now realize she wasn't doing it for the money because her family was well off. Her family had just arrived in town and already opened a unique variety store. It was unique because it was the first and only store to sell American apples and grapes. By writing for me, she could gain access to my answers in class. However, at the time, if she was kind enough to offer then I wasn't going to pass up on the deal. The teachers knew about my conditions, and they knew I was an exceptional student—both in my deportment and academic performance—I just struggled to write.

For weeks, I went without a lunch every day. Many days, I could hardly walk the mile and a half home from school. I was so hungry that my stomach went into a growling overdrive. One particular evening, I lingered behind in the schoolyard since I could not keep up with the other kids making the same journey home. As I walked home by myself, I prayed to God asking him to not let me faint, and he delivered. I saw my Aunty V standing in front of her restaurant. I ran and hugged her. She was so glad to see me, but I was more excited to see her. She took me inside and we walked through the restaurant to the back where she resided. She asked me what I wanted to eat, and I was never so relieved to see food away from home.

After that evening, I no longer walked back home with my school peers. Instead, I stopped by my Aunty V's restaurant most evenings and ate, and then she would ask one of her patrons to give me a ride home. My grandmother, Ma B, noticed and asked why I was stopping by the restaurant each evening. I told her that I was hungry, and I needed to eat. However, she wasn't convinced I was telling her the full story, so she sat me down and made me explain everything to her. When I was finished, she said nothing and just walked away. I prayed to God hoping she wouldn't spoil things by telling me to come straight home after school. Every time I asked God for help, I had to wait awhile but He always came through for me. What He was about to do for me, a little seven-year-old girl, was beyond comprehension at the time, and only years after do I understand the depth of his compassion towards me.

My Grandfather called me into the bedroom that night and asked me to repeat the story I told my grandmother. My heart sank; however, I did. My grandfather, affectionately called Mr. Bob, was a man of few words. After working on the sugar estate as an overseer, he would come home to relax—with a Red Stripe beer and a Matterhorn cigarette in hand. Often, he would be sitting on a stool by the side of the house singing his favorite song, "Draw Me Nearer." The song was so sweet and melodious to my ears that I had memorized it, and this song became my rock in later years. After I recounted my story, I stood by his bedside rubbing my hands together. He turned to look at me. He smiled, and then said, "I am going to help you write."

During the next couple of weeks, my grandfather would hold my hand with the pencil and help me form each letter into words. We would start at 7:00 p.m. and continue until 9:00 p.m. We would use the light from the kerosene lamp with the Home Sweet Home lamp shade. It was difficult at times, but I became more relaxed under his guidance. Writing was a big part of his day-to-day tasks on the estate. He would write down each laborer's name and the amount of work they got, so to him writing came so naturally. In later years, he told me that my plight at school had brought him to tears the first time he heard about it from Ma B, and he knew then that he had to help me. And with his help, I built up my confidence. I could master the task of writing.

When I had more confidence, I decided to write on my own for the first time in so long. I was ready as I had practiced by myself all weekend. I sat smiling in class on Monday morning. I told my paid writer that I had no money. Nonetheless, she still offered to do it, but I said, "No." I could feel her eyes on me as I copied the work from the blackboard and filled in the correct answers. I had a firm grip on the coco-cola pencil, and I finished my writing before the bell rang. I was no longer the struggling child. With my grandfather's help, I did it! I placed my head on the desk and cried with joy at my accomplishment.

CHAPTER TWO

My own hell on earth

I loved school, and I was a good scholar. However, surviving daily was challenging. A renewed confidence was born within me. If I could overcome one of my most difficult situations at such a young age, then I told myself, 'I could do anything.' But just as I was beginning to be accepted and loved for who I was, fate dealt me another trial. I was still being taunted. I was still being teased and laughed at, but I had older friends, Vicky, Beverley, Judy, and Hope, who would take me away as soon as my peers descended on me. They were my elders, and they were always looking out for the smaller kids. To them, I will forever be grateful.

When I was in the third grade, I loved to sit at the back of the class. I was the most comfortable there since no one would stare at me when I held my hand up to answer a question. I felt as if I needed to answer every question because I already knew the answers. However, the teacher would skip over me just to give the other students a chance to answer, but if they didn't get it right then she would call upon me. Those were proud moments for me. But I still struggled with being fully accepted.

One day, I was sitting in class when I felt someone hit me through the window. In response, I immediately closed the window. As I stepped out of the classroom that afternoon, I saw Gean and instantly knew he was the culprit. He was a very large guy, who everyone was afraid of. As I slowly walked past him, he grabbed me by my collar and started slapping my face, and then he ran off in a flash. That was the beginning of my daily beating from Gean. He would use his fists to strike me, and his open hands to slap me. At times, four or five other kids had to intervene just to get me away from him. As his forceful blows struck me, I would holler so loudly you could hear me from a mile away. Why was he doing this to me? Was it because I was one of the most vulnerable kids and couldn't defend myself? One evening, I was running away from him and fell in the street—bruising my knees. My friend, Alva, came and picked me up. His mother, Miss Hearstcey, cleaned my wounds and comforted me. I was shaking uncontrollably and thought I was going to die. "Why me, Lord?"

After reporting the incident to the local police station, Ma B came to my school. The principal, Bend Pipe, as he was nicknamed, told the detective he had no knowledge of me being beaten by this bully. However, Gean was warned by both the detective and the principal to stay away from me. Thank goodness! He never laid his hands on me again. When I became an adult, I went by the store where he worked to ask him why he had done that to me. To my surprise, his response was, "Because I liked you."

My confidence was growing. I felt confident to start engaging my peers in conversation, which was how I won them over. Now, they were my friends. I no longer cried at school. Whenever they called me "Shaky" or something else, I blocked them out. I was now in control.

After a while, everyone wanted to be my friend. I had an infectious laugh, and I became a fun person to be around. I was also knowledgeable about world leaders like Israel's Prime Minister, Benjamin Netanyahu; Iran's leader, Ayatollah Khomeini; and Cuba's Prime Minister, Fidel Castro. I remembered facts about the war fought by the Russians and Afghanistan peoples. I could also quote world leaders. I think I was the only one who listened to the BBC world news broadcast (which was what was available to us at the time) since I knew so much about what was happening in the world. I knew my new friends didn't have a clue about some of the world events I was talking about. They often questioned my "foreign tales," so I shared with them what I knew and spent time explaining everything. It felt good being knowledgeable. Soon, everyone was asking me for advice or simply for me to tell them about something they didn't know.

Weekends were my favorite times. Every Saturday morning at 5:30 a.m., Ma B and I would listen to the Oral Roberts healing broadcast on the radio from Minneapolis, Minnesota, USA. She would have me touch the radio on the dresser "as a point of contact," as she firmly believed his prayers would heal me "from the crown of my head to the soles of my feet."

"Live Study Fellowship" was another Christian organization Ma B was fond of. She requested prayers of healing for me from them too. On Sundays, I went to Sunday school followed by Praise and Worship services, and then the Youth fellowship at the Annotto Bay Baptist Church. That church was where I met lasting friends. And it was also my faith in God and earnestness to worship him that led me to a life-changing experience.

CHAPTER THREE

Finding and accepting myself

My best friend, Jennifer, was like my sister. She lived on the outskirts of town in a place called 'Marking Stone.' I lived a few blocks away by the Railway Crossing, and close to the sea in a little house owned by Grays' Inn Sugar Plantations.

Every morning, we woke up to the sounds of the waves as they dashed ashore splashing on the sands. It was such a beautiful sight, especially looking on at the horizon where the sea seems to meet the sky. Those sights—along with the warm atmosphere and peaceful surroundings—were the only positives to this little village for me. Marking Stone only had a few decent houses, and Jennifer lived in one with her parents. Their house had three bedrooms, a large living and dining room, and a bathroom with modern plumbing. In contrast, I still bathed in an outside bathroom and used an outhouse. I often wondered if my grandparents were ever going to be able to build a decent bathroom. I was so afraid of using the outhouse, especially if nature called during the night. The other houses in the area were run-down shacks rented to drifters who were passing through.

There were a few people who had settled in the area. Some of whom did odd jobs in the adjoining town.

Even as a small child, I often wondered if this was really what my life was going to be like. It was like the poorest of the poor. Jennifer and I would talk about what we wanted to be when we grew up even though we knew nothing of the outside world. We were already dreaming and planning our escape. However, I was very mindful that sometimes even the best planning can still be derailed—leaving you trapped in a place or situation. Sometimes, due to no fault of your own.

Like most small villages, this one also had its own characters. Poppy was the wise old man, who told old wives' tales. Everyone in my neighborhood loved and respected him. You could sit and listen to him for hours just telling stories of the past. Shoey was the singer, who sang at "Nine Nights,"—an age-old traditional event that was held nine days after a person died. He could sing just like my grandfather. They both hailed from the Parish of Clarendon. They both came to St. Mary's Parish as part of the "Nine Nights" band as singers, and afterward, they settled in the Parish. Poppy and Shoey were always together. Then there was Mammy, who was a short old lady. She was the shopkeeper's mother, who wanted to know everyone's business before she allowed her daughter to extend credit for any provisions. As a small child, I was told to treat everyone with the utmost respect. I was told to always say, "Yes, Sir; No, Sir; Yes, Miss; No, Miss." And as a child, you obeyed your elders. However, this old lady always left me with an unfavorable opinion. I had to pass by her each time I went by Jennifer's house, but I always refused to look at her. No one liked her.

Jennifer and I started studying for the Technical High school examinations. She would come by my house one day and I would go by hers the next day. We earnestly studied and were confident in our ability to pass the exam. On the morning of the exam, I woke up, ate my breakfast, got dressed, and waited for Jennifer outside my house. Suddenly, I started crying. I cried so much that Ma B had to hold me up. A lady in her car stopped to ask what was going on and Ma B explained to her that I was nervous about taking the exam that morning. I can still hear the lady's voice asking Ma B, "Did you say your prayers this morning?"

"Yes," came the answer. However, I never took the exam. When the results came out, Jennifer had passed the exam and was going to attend Dunhill Technical High School in St. Catherine's Parish. To this day, I'm still unable to explain what came over me that morning. I asked God to show me or give me an answer; however, I received no answer. This was the first of many unexplainable events that plagued my life.

The new school year was approaching, and Ma B said I was going to attend a new school called Windsor Castle All Age which was about 5.5 miles from my home. I would have to take the bus to and from school. I wondered where the money would be coming from for the bus fare. However, I didn't have a say in the decision regarding the school. It was already decided. When Ma B took me to get registered, I immediately fell in love with the school. It was much smaller than my previous school, but the empty classrooms looked warm and inviting. I knew I was going to excel in a smaller setting.

The principal, "Man Teacher" as he was affectionately called, walked with a limp and a cane which he called "the rod of correction." His wife, Miss T, was also a teacher there. She oversaw the Private Lessons program. They had three daughters: Karren, Mary, and Juliet. One of their daughters, Karri, as she was affectionately called, was born with some deformities. I could see that her parents were very protective of her. After registration, we went home. I couldn't wait to start the semester. I loved everything about the school. It was also a big relief that the bus stop was right there, and I didn't have to walk to school anymore.

On my first day of school, I met Peggy R. I caught her staring at me, so I smiled at her. She walked over and introduced herself. I instantly liked her. That same day we walked across the street and bought our lunches together. Soon, Peggy R was introducing me to all her friends. However, I was drawn to Marcia A. She was Peggy's best friend and was drawn to me as well. I felt so happy with my newfound friends. I anticipated that I would have a good time at my new school and thanked God for answering my prayers.

My new school was heaven. Some children would stare at me, but not many of them taunted me. The taunters were the ones from my old school and a few others liked to join in. A few would shout, "Shaky!" from afar, but I never acknowledged them as I had more friends than not in this new school. For the most part, the other students showed maturity and empathy. I made friends and established some lasting friendships. I excelled in this new environment, and a new wave of confidence was born within me. I learned to control my shaking when I could and learned to be more me too. This was a life-changing experience for me—so profoundly was this experience rooted in my dream to be counted, seen, and be a contributing member of society. It was at this school, Windsor Castle All Age, that I found myself, and in doing so I found peace.

CHAPTER FOUR

Maturity and Family at long last

In 1969, a new Secondary School was scheduled to open at Kildare about 1.5 miles from Buff Bay, Portland. Some of the students at school, including me, were going to be transferred there. I was thirteen years old by then, and ready for another challenge. I missed my friend, Jennifer, but accepted the fact that nothing really lasts forever. I enjoyed my last school term at Windsor Castle All Age and cherished the time I spent there with Peggy and my other friends.

Summer was fast approaching, and I looked forward to it. That summer was a lazy one. I had a daily ritual of going by the beach in the early mornings to watch the fishermen row in their boats. I was always excited to watch the hauls. Sometimes, they caught a good number of fish. Sometimes, not at all. These fishermen were relentless. They went out every night to make their livelihood. My favorite fisherman was Papa Son. He was dark, strong, and hardly spoke. He was also a good singer and a kind man. Then, there was Joe Cahn. He was a short Indian man who walked with a hunch. He was jovial and kind. Most times, onlookers came just to see if they could get a few fish for their dinner, especially those with kids. The fish that weren't for sale were given away. I never knew why some of the fish weren't for sale, but back then, we were all too happy to get the leftovers.

I was always fascinated by the sea—the blue color, the waves, the small boats moving to the sea's rhythm, and just the water lapping at my feet. The solace I found being near the sea was incredible. I would read by the beach, and my imagination would run wild. I would write most of my future award-winning poetry in the early hours at this beach. The inspiration would flow like a river with my hands trying to quickly write down the words of a poetic song, a romantic poem, or everyday life tales that streamed from my brain. The sea brought me solace and helped to shape my path as an award-winning writer. So yes, during the summer my time by the sea was indeed special.

However, it was September morning before I knew it. The new school, Buff Bay Secondary, in the small district of Kildare was 10 miles from my house. I was back to traveling to school again. The school was a large and beautiful two-story building. When we gathered for Devotion and the Welcome Speech, I noticed some of my friends from Windsor Castle All Age School were there, and even kids from my first school. I loved my new uniform—a white blouse with a sky blue, straight fitted skirt and navy-blue socks with black shoes. When I saw myself in the mirror, I felt like I looked so grown. I loved the image of myself that stared back at me.

A small shop stood adjacent to the school's buildings. Miss P was the sole proprietor. She had a beautiful soul. Her daughter, Via, had an infectious smile that could brighten up any dull day. However, I was drawn to her son, Richie, who was in my class. Miss P soon became a mother figure to everyone. She loved us and was loved right back. The school had a cafeteria and a tuck shop, but Miss P catered to the kids. She sold what kids craved. And if you were a couple cents short on your purchase, she would still give you what you wanted. The school principal, Mr. Dennis, was very tall and lanky. His wife, Mrs. Dennis, who had a medium build with long hair flowing down her shoulders, was the assistant principal. To me, they complemented each other.

The two years at this school helped me in my growth development. I knew I had neurological disorders, but there was no diagnosis to support this. I still shook at times but not like before. I realized when I was upset, I would shake more, so it was in my own interest to always keep calm. I learned to be easygoing. I marveled at how far I had come—from my first day at primary school to now—at this school with other wonderful students.

It was exam time again, and we had to choose which high school we wanted to attend. The choices were Titchfield High School or Port Antonio Technical Institute. When the decision was made, I was placed at the Port Antonio Technical Institute. The decision wasn't favorable. I had no clue as to why I ended up at that school, but I decided I was going to make the most of my opportunity. The school building was on the compound of Port Antonio High School—formerly known as Port Antonio Secondary. I was now traveling twenty-eight miles to school.

During my time there, something very disturbing was going on with the young schoolgirls and the school bus drivers. To clarify, these buses were not provided by the school. They were buses from the Victor/Mail bus company based in Kingston. One bus route was from Kingston to Port Antonio; the second bus route was the Port Maria Special, which plied the route from Port Maria to Port Antonio. These buses were the main vehicles for transportation to and from school.

One of the bus drivers, Roy, was handsome, charismatic, and had a wicked smile. All the older girls were crazy about him. There were even rumors about some girls getting pregnant by him—and some of those allegations later turned out to be true. This was only the beginning of something that would change my life forever.

I stood at the bus stop one afternoon minding my own business when Roy walked over to me. "Hi, pretty girl." He said with his trademark smile.

I looked him up and down. "Hi," I said. "Is it true?"

"Is what true?" He asked.

"That you are getting all these girls pregnant?" I responded.

"It's not true." He said and walked away.

At this institution, I learned commercial subjects, such as typewriting, shorthand writing, and Accounting and Business Management. I met three friends there: Ronica, Maize, and Violet. I loved the classes except for Shorthand Writing. I wasn't good at typing because my hands would visibly shake during the typing tests. I asked my mom for a typewriter, and she sent me a Royal Model Typewriter. I was so happy I could practice at home at my own pace.

My friends and I sat together, studied together, had lunch together, and had fun together. I loved these guys, and we formed a bond that I will forever hold dear to my heart. Maize became my writing partner. We wrote essays and entered writing competitions together. We both won our fair share of awards. And whenever she came to spend the weekend with me, we would stay up until the wee hours of the morning writing short stories and poems. We wrote about love, friendship, and happiness. We stretched our imagination to places where words came alive. Maize soon became my best friend.

I was approaching sixteen years old, and yet, I felt empty because I didn't know much about my dad. I was yearning to learn about him. I often wondered why he had never reached out to me or even tried to find me. My grandfather knew I was sad because I didn't know my father. He knew where to find my father but ignored my pleas. Ma B, on the other hand, tried to comfort me whenever I would get upset about the subject. Finally, my grandfather reached out to someone who was a relative of my father via mail for a meetup. We were all awaiting his reply. When I got home one evening, I was greeted with the news that my grandfather had heard from my father and that he had sent money for me to come visit him. Ma B decided to take me the following weekend. I was so happy; I could hardly contain myself. Finally, I was on my way to meet him with Ma B. During the long bus ride from Kingston to May Pen, Clarendon; I enjoyed the scenery and chatted with Ma B about my fears of being rejected by my new family. She assured me that everything was going to be alright.

We arrived early that Saturday morning at Race Course, Clarendon. I met my grand aunt for the first time when we stopped by her grocery store. After years of my growing sadness about not knowing my father and the nagging questions I asked about him, my grandfather finally decided to reach out to my grand aunt, who then contacted my father and made this meeting possible. I hugged her warmly.

"I remember your mom," was the first thing she said to me. As she prepared refreshments for us, I couldn't help myself. "Where is my father?" She just smiled at me and continued what she was doing. As I gazed out the open window, I saw a man getting off a red Yamaha bike. I took one more look at him, and I knew instantly that he was my father. He awkwardly walked towards the door. As he entered, I eagerly ran towards him, and he scooped me up in his arms. I thought my heart would burst open. I was so glad to finally be meeting the man, who had eluded me for close to sixteen years. Pops, as he was affectionately called, could not contain the tears rolling down his cheeks. He continued to look me over and say, "You are so pretty." He ran his hands through my long, black hair, and placed tiny kisses on my cheeks. It was so wonderful to meet my father at long last.

Our second stop was at a bar owned by one of my aunts. She was so delighted to see me. The men in the bar all turned toward me as my father announced me, "This is my daughter." One man shouted from the back, "Where is the other one?" He knew I was a twin, and he was asking for my sibling. My father's family was all glad to see me, but I didn't have time to take it all in. At another house, we stopped to meet another aunt. She was warm and offered us refreshments, but I was full so dad told her that he would bring me back over later that night.

I visited my father's house and thought he was poorer than me. However, as I looked at the nearby outhouse, I noticed construction work was going on besides the house. He must have seen the puzzled look on my face because he said, "I am building my house over there." I replied, "Nice." While at my father's, I met my sister, my two brothers, and my stepmother. My siblings seemed sincerely happy to see me. I was so excited to show up and be a part of their family. Ma B was lost in all this, but she took no offense as she was genuinely happy for me. We had a wonderful time and even went to meet some of my mother's family. Meeting my father was a very fulfilling experience. Oh, the joy that washed over me left me with memories that will last a lifetime.

CHAPTER FIVE

The Secret: The half that has never been told

It was back to my old life; however, my life seemed brighter now. Suddenly, I had a father with a whole extended family. All the festive activities might have been what caused my period to come for the first time—two weeks before my sixteenth birthday. When I was almost fifteen, Ma B took me to the doctor because I hadn't yet gotten a period. The doctor said, "Not to worry, she's just a late starter." Now, it was here. Hello! My birthday came, and as usual Ma B baked me a cake and bought ice cream. We sat in the early evening sun—shooting the breeze and eating cake. It was real fun.

At school, I was becoming popular. I think it was because I was a fun person, and very intellectual in certain areas. I excelled in writing. One of my teachers even suggested that maybe I should pursue a career in journalism. After that conversation, I considered a career in journalism because I knew I wanted to be a writer, and I was determined to achieve that goal. I was the happiest at school because I could learn so much.

Apart from my school, there were two other high schools: Portland High (which was a private school operated by the Seventh Day Adventist Church) and Titchfield High School. I had friends from both schools because we all travelled to and from school on the same bus. On my ride home in the evenings, I would usually volunteer to help collect fares from passengers on the bus. This led to a friendship with the conductress, Clara K. She was always pleasant and fun to be around. Clara K always invited me to spend the weekend with her daughter; I always told her that Ma B wouldn't let me.

One evening, I asked again, and Ma B said, "Yes, as long as your friend discusses it with me and asks for my permission." Two weeks later, Clara K was throwing a birthday party for her daughter, so that was the perfect time for me to spend the weekend with her. I was so excited as I had never been to a sweet sixteen party before nor someone else's house for a weekend.

Clara K and I arrived at her house. She showed me to my room, and I unpacked my bags. I looked at the nightdress my mom had sent from London and held it close to my chest. The sweet smell of lavender perfume came from the fabric. I was tired but couldn't sleep. This was too much! I couldn't believe I was in Kingston about to attend a real party. Wow! The next morning, I met her daughter, Kandy C. She was stunning. There was beauty all over her. She was excited about her party. We drove with her mom to the hairdresser at the Twin Gates Mall on Constant Spring Road. After we left the parlor, we did some window shopping while her mom picked up the cake. On our arrival back to her home, I saw some of her friends sitting on the verandah playing cards. They looked me over before she could get a chance to introduce me; however, when she introduced me, they all sincerely hugged me.

The long living room was decorated with streamers in blue, white, and light purple. The balloons were the same colors. There was a bar to the far right, and a DJ was outside on the verandah. I asked Kandy C earlier what my role was going to be, and she told me, "Meet and greet the guests." I got dressed and put on my best smile. I was ready to meet the night, but I was not ready for what the night had in store for me. Help me, Lord!

The party was a blast, and everyone had a good time. I got complimented on my hair and my smile. When I had a break, I would go to the bar to grab a tonic water. When the party was winding down in the wee hours, I went to the bar, got my drink, and as I stepped away someone called out my name. I turned around, and there he stood grinning at me with that smile. It was no other than Roy—the handsome bus driver with a bad reputation.

"You look so good. Come and have a drink with me." He said.

"Thanks, but I can't," I said, and just walked away as he stared at me.

I wasn't surprised to see him. I knew more than likely he would be here since he and Clara K often worked together. He never even had a conversation with me after I asked him about the other girls. Why was he now asking me to have a drink with him?

I walked back to the other girls. They were engaged in a conversation about the cute boys at their school. A few of the boys were in attendance at the party. There was this guy named Josh who caught my eyes. He cut the cake with Kandy C. I later learned he had a crush on her, but she wasn't interested in boys just yet. The party was over, and I retired to bed.

In the early hours, I was awakened by Clara K saying, "Roy wants to talk to you." I thought it was strange he wanted to talk to me at that time of the night, but I got out of bed and followed her to the porch where he sat drinking a Red Stripe beer.

"What?" I curtly asked.

"Sit," he said. "I want to talk to you."

I sat on the vacant chair beside him.

"My friends were inquiring about you, and I told them you were my girlfriend." He said.

Stunned by his statement, I asked, "How old are you?" He didn't respond. I lied and said, "Furthermore, I have a boyfriend." The moment those words left my lips I regretted them.

My answer caught him by surprise as he inquired, "Really?" Before I could answer and correct myself, he changed the subject. "Why do we have to wait on you most mornings? Why can't you get dressed and be outside like the other students?"

I looked at him and asked, "What are you talking about? I don't even take your bus."

"But I know about your tardiness, everyone talks about it." He said. However, I knew that wasn't true. He was just trying to get back at me for what I had talked to him about a month earlier.

He smiled, "Let's go talk in the car. I want to show you something."

I shook my head. "Let's talk tomorrow. I am very tired and need to go back to bed. However, he insisted on showing me something in his car. I reluctantly walked with him to the car and sat in the passenger seat. He turned on the radio, and I felt relaxed listening to the music.

Suddenly, he drove off. "I'm going to show you a great scenery. You're going to see the city below."

My heart sank. This wasn't good. I pleaded with him to take me back, but he just continued driving. He suddenly stopped and turned the car engine off. Before I could catch my breath, he was like a wild animal. He began ripping off my nightgown. I started to scream, "Stop! Stop! No! No!" I tried hitting him in the face, but he was too strong for me. All I could think of was how much I loathed him, and that this bastard was going to rape me. He entered me with such force that all I could do was scream some more as he took control of my body. It seemed like an eternity, but then he climaxed. Then, nothing.

Suddenly, there was a knock on the window. As I looked up, I saw a cop standing beside the car. As Roy wound down the window, the cop asked him to step outside. When the officer interrogated him, he lied. He said

I was his girlfriend, and that he wasn't raping me. We were just having rough sex.

"Look, officer, she is in her nightgown."

To my horror, the officer just walked away. To this day, I don't understand why I didn't stand up to him. I blame myself for not telling the officer the truth, but I guess I was in shock. I was so devastated and tried to comprehend the gravity of what really happened. I was so distraught and frightened. I didn't know where I was. I cried all the way back to the house. He let himself in, and I somehow stumbled to the room I was staying in. I saw my reflection in the mirror and didn't recognize the stranger staring back at me. I looked at my ripped nightgown stained with blood, curled up in a fetal position on the floor, and wept.

I heard a knock then the door opened, and Clara K walked in. "What the fuck happened to you?" She dropped to the floor beside me and began rocking me back and forth.

I held my face up and stared at her with hot, burning tears washing over my face. "How could you do this to me? How could you Clara? You woke me up and threw me to a predator in waiting. Why? You were supposed to protect me."

She took me to the bathroom. I stood under the shower trying to scrub the dirt and slime off my body. 'This was all a bad dream, and I was going to wake up from it.'

The next day I stayed in bed. I didn't want to eat or drink anything—I just wanted to die. Later in the day, Roy came to see me.

"I am so sorry," he said. "I didn't know you were a virgin. You told me you had a boyfriend." I looked at him with contempt and disgust. "I had fallen in love with you," he stated.

"Why are you here? To rape me again?" I asked. "I will make it easier for you this time." I left the bed and started removing my clothes. He just got up and walked away.

How could this happen to me? I didn't move in his circle. The high school girls he ran around with weren't even my friends. I wasn't friendly with him. How could I end up being a statistic?

The shame, guilt, and regret of not being able to defend myself against this beast washed over me once more. I turned my head to the wall and started sobbing. Then, the shaking returned. 'Oh, God, no, please. I am going to die. Dear God, don't let me die without seeing Ma B.' These thoughts raced through my mind.

I felt weak and nauseous. I hadn't eaten all day, so I thought maybe I was dehydrated and was about to faint. I sat in a daze—motionless and scared. What if I never see my grandmother again? "Oh, Ma B, where are you?" I whispered in the darkness of the room. Finally, the shaking subsided but my hands were still visibly shaking. Clara K walked in with food and drinks on a tray. When I held the glass to my lips, my hands shook so badly that she had to help me.

She was surprised to see me like this. "What did he do to you?"

As if it wasn't obvious. "I want to go home." She wrapped her arms around me and hugged me. It felt comforting but only for a moment. Then I lashed out, "Take me home. I don't want to die here!"

The next morning, I was supposed to be dressed in uniform for school, and then I would stop by my house, drop my bag off and continue to school. Instead, I just dressed in the same clothes I wore Friday.

"Aren't you going to school?" Clara K asked.

I just looked at her—in awe of her stupidity.

I sat at the back of the bus trying to avoid my peers who would be boarding for school. Clara K and I remained relatively cold towards each other. In my heart, I believed she had betrayed me by waking me up and putting me in that situation. Although, I will forever blame myself for getting into the car with him. I did so because I felt comfortable at that moment in his company. I didn't like his reputation, but what he did to me was the furthest thing from my mind. Not in my wildest dreams could I have imagined that. Now, I had to see his face almost every freaking day, and the anger began to boil within me. He was a big, grown-ass man, and I was just sixteen. I wasn't a typical sixteen-year-old either. I had my medical issues and other issues to deal with, and this was the last and worst thing that could ever happen to me. But why me?

The bus stopped at my house, and I got off. I saw Ma B, and I just wrapped my arms around her. A few girls were calling out to me, but I was caught up in the moment with the one I loved the most.

CHAPTER SIX

Needing and Finding Triple Strength

I told Ma B everything. I told her, "It was just the thought of seeing you and grandpa again that helped me to get through."

Ma B was ready to confront both of them. She was also ready to go to the police station to make a report and have him arrested. I tried to reason with her, and let her see it from my point of view. I didn't want this to become a scandal because of the medical condition I had. I was the one who would suffer the most. I began to cry all over again. I just couldn't get the thought of him on top of me and hurting me out of my mind—it kept playing over and over again. I knew deep in my heart that Clara K knew exactly what had happened to me, but I told Ma B that I hadn't admitted anything to her, and he wouldn't either.

"So, this will be our secret."

She looked at me for what seemed like an eternity, and then asked, "between whom?" I forced a smile. "You and Me."

She wiped the tears from my eyes. We embraced, and then she said, "Let's eat."

It was about 9:30 a.m. when I went to use the bathroom and felt a burning sensation in my vagina. I thought it was because I felt so sore down there already. But when I went again later, I knew that it was much more. I knew he not only raped me and took away the most precious thing a girl held dear, her virginity, but that he also had left me with an STD.

I had to go see Dr. Martin to confirm this. I tried to relax a little, but I could see the worried look on Ma B's face. I told her, "If my suspicion is true, then this is something curable."

Then she broke down crying. "This is too much my child. This is going to break you," she sobbed.

"I am already broken, Ma B. I am already broken."

I quickly dried the hot tears rolling down my face and walked into my room. I had no idea where the money was going to come from. Suddenly, I had an idea. I called out to her. "We will go to the doctor tomorrow afternoon just before closing." I knew my poor grandmother didn't have the money for the doctor's visit, but I came up with a plan.

We would go to the town square and await Roy. Ma B knew she couldn't face him without attacking him, and I didn't want her looking into that bastard's face, so I told her I would handle the situation. His bus rode in, and before he even had a chance to alight—I was right there. He was surprised to see me. Before he could say anything, I spoke. I wasted no time.

"I need to see the doctor. I need money for the visit and to fill a prescription if deemed necessary."

"Okay, I'll let you have it in the morning."

"In the morning, you are going to put it in an envelope, place it in a book and your pimp will take it to Ma B."

"Can I talk to you for a second?"

"We have nothing to talk about." I flatly replied.

As I was leaving, Clara K walked up to me and asked, "Are you ok?"

I just ignored her and walked away.

The next morning Clara K brought the book to Ma B. I looked at her in anger. Then, he came out to ask why I wasn't going to school. I drew him close to me and whispered in his ears, "Because you gave me an STD, mother fucker." He just stood there, and I walked back to my house.

After doing a series of tests, it was confirmed that I had contracted an STD. Dr. Martin asked Ma B to step outside while he questioned me. It was during our conversation in his office that I accepted I wasn't to be blamed for the rape, and I didn't have to go through life with this burden of guilt or believing it was my fault. I couldn't help asking, "Why me?" I had come through so much already, and now this was tormenting my soul. Later that evening, I locked myself away and cried. I cried and cried some more. What did I do in my young life to deserve this? I wasn't given the chance to give myself freely to whom I pleased. I had lost my innocence and my trust in people. I had worked so hard trying to overcome my disability, and just when I thought I had put most of my emotional baggage to rest—this happened. I had to find a way to go on. I was either going to succumb to the brutality of this rape and its aftermath by having a nervous breakdown or I was going to continue working on overcoming my disability. I choose the latter.

As I dressed for school, I made a choice. I was going to lock away this ugliness and focus on my well-being. It was good to be in class again. I acted normal, but deep inside my heart was breaking into a trillion prices. However, I survived the day, and I knew then that I would survive many more days. I had my whole life ahead of me, and with God's help, I would get through this.

After my two years at Port Antonio Technical Institute, I thought of looking for a job. When I was only seventeen, I enrolled in Whyte's Business College. I became "Head Girl," and quickly gained the respect of the other students. My shaking and volatile emotions were under control. I learned how to have fun in this new environment. At this school, I also learned how to be a leader. I performed my role accordingly. I became fearless in all things. I was no longer that scared, helpless child trapped in a car with a man fucking my brains out. No, I had risen from the depth of those dark moments to great heights of light.

My God filled me with strength, and my mind and body prospered from such a gift. Amen.

CHAPTER SEVEN

My sweet bitter love

It was almost time to graduate from Whyte's Business College. There was nothing more to learn there. The next step was to find myself a job. I couldn't wait to get a job. I started sending out my resume to different government agencies and different companies in the private sector—hoping to be called for an interview. I crossed my fingers and waited.

That following weekend, Ma B said someone had asked her for permission to date me and she had said yes. She continued, "He's a good man for you, and you should get to know him." By now, I was over eighteen, so this must have been someone from my old school. But why did Ma B see the need for me to date this man? I really wasn't ready for any of that just yet. Some nights, I still had nightmares. I would relive the nightmare repeatedly, and it kept me up at night. Why would he want to date me anyway?

Later that evening, my prospective date arrived. I just stood there staring at him. He wasn't a stranger. I knew him

45

and wasn't surprised to see him. George was a decent man. He was more on the quiet side, and he also had a daughter. He, too, was raised by his grandmother. We sat down to talk while Ma B brought us refreshments. He told me that he had been accepted into the Police Academy and would be leaving shortly for training.

The next day, there was a cricket match at the Grays' Inn by the cricket club. Ma B was the head cook—as she always was for these occasions. She was a good cook, and they paid her well. George and I went to see the match. This was our first official date. It was cool. Later, we kissed for the first time. It was the first time I was kissing a man. I didn't know how to act.

Three weeks after our first date, he left. I really missed his company. We began sending scores of love letters—professing our undying love for each other. I had just started to identify with my emotions. I knew I might love him, but I was not in love with him. I had yet to experience the magic of it. Maybe I was closing myself up inside. Maybe I wasn't yet ready to let love in. Despite my real feelings about George, I promised I would wait for him. I wrote that we could get married after he graduated from the Police Academy. What could ever go wrong?

After that letter, weeks passed by. I didn't think much about it. I continued with my life. And one evening on my way home, I saw a guy who I instantly liked. Just like that. Were my emotions playing with me? The next day, I asked my friend, Dory, about him. She told me his name was Craig. When I told her I wanted to meet him, she just laughed at me. I was dead serious, but she brushed me off. For the first time ever, I went to bed with a guy on my mind. I had to see him again up close, and maybe personal.

The following week, Dory and I went out for lunch and bumped into him. That was when Dory told him I was asking about him. He flashed me a smile, and I introduced myself. He introduced himself too. Dory said she thought I was joking all this time. I just smiled at her in response. I didn't know then that this was going to be the beginning of my loving and giving relationship. The closest thing to heaven.

After meeting Craig, I also met and hit it off with one of Craig's sisters, Marva. I knew then that I was now ready to see what love was all about. I feared ending up in bed with him at some point, but I was ready to meet that challenge. I no longer dwelt on the rape. I wasn't healed from it, but I was going to live my life as I saw fit. It was almost two years later, and during that time I had built up my physical strength. I had conditioned my mind to be able to do anything, and I drew closer to my God. He had always been my rock—a shelter in the times of all my storms. Despite my challenges, I gave him praises for his many blessings, and the compassion he bestowed on me.

I finally began to see the world in terms of love and falling in love. But first, I had to make the coast clear. I wrote to George. I told him I was calling off our relationship. I told him I wasn't ready. He came to see me that weekend. We talked and talked, but I was done. It really pained me to look him in the eyes because I knew he was a good man who didn't deserve to have his heart broken. A still, small voice as if from an angel told me that I was making a big mistake, but I didn't listen.

My job hunting paid off; I got a job at Port Antonio Secondary School. I was hired to teach business education to tenth and eleventh graders. I was excited! This was my first job. It was going to be challenging, yet I was going to meet the challenge. I was also already poised for all life had to offer. I was just a couple years older than the kids, but I was going to put my shoulders to the wheel and do my best. I was entrusted to teach them, and business education was my best academic achievement to date.

God had been so good to me. Only a true and living God could have taken me to this point. I hadn't gone to a teacher's college, yet I was given this tremendous opportunity. I choked back tears on my first day on the job. How could this happen to me? I went home that night feeling vindicated. Yes, I had amounted to something in life. Thanks to Ma B, my second mother, and grandpa P. I hugged them that night, and we cried together. I had come a long way—fighting all the obstacles that dared to hold me back. I gathered all my strength. With the help of God, I was going to make it.

CHAPTER EIGHT

No greater love ♥

My new boyfriend, Craig, was amazing in every way. The relationship was super exciting, and I was very happy. I knew Craig had another woman, but to me, it was okay because he wasn't married, and she lived in another parish. Ma B was so upset. Actually, I should say she was downright mad about all this and warned me that this would be my biggest mistake. "How could you give up a man who loved you for a player?" she scolded. I tuned her out. My sweet, Ma B, who I loved second to none was now getting on my nerves because she was against the relationship. She refused to meet him, and that created an antagonizing relationship between us. However, I was not going to be deterred. The more she bad-mouthed him—the more I went to see him.

I was in love, and I felt somewhat liberated from my past emotional pains. This was my healing. I was past the point of return—no amount of reasoning could have convinced me to give up Craig. I clung to him like peas in a pod.

I never knew sex could be so satisfying and glorious. Craig was a wonderful teacher in that area, and I tried very hard to master the art. At one point, I was just lost in all the sexual activities. I learned from Craig what making love was all about. The first time we made love I noticed the puzzled look on his face when he saw the bloodstain on the bed linens. Why were the linens stained? I gathered my clothes and headed for the bathroom. I knew what he was thinking—which was further from the truth. He was not my first, and I was not a virgin.

The relationship was flourishing, but something was amiss. I tried reasoning it away, but it was always there staring me in the face. In truth, Ma B was right. Craig was a player. He was a womanizer. He was always moving around in different circles because his past relationships never stayed in the past. To this day, I still can't fathom why I stayed with him especially when I had so much going on for me but stay I did. Maybe I stayed for fear of leaving and not knowing what I would get myself into after our relationship was over? Maybe I believed he would love me enough to change his wild ways? But that was an illusion. There was always a constant string of women, who came floating in and out of his life, at one point or another during our relationship. Some of his encounters were just short-lived slings while others were more lingering. Yet through it all, I stayed and suffered so much emotional pain.

One weekend, Craig and I went to Montego Bay. The trip was fun filled. That Sunday as I was enjoying the ride home a young lady approached me. She told me she was his baby's mother. After that surprise, she said she didn't know how I was going to handle their situation; however, she wanted me to know that she wasn't leaving Craig. After that encounter, I told Craig to put his baby momma on a leash as I wasn't going to be disrespected. In retrospect, I should have walked away then, but I was too caught up in the excitement of being with Craig, and feeding my cravings for love, so much so, that I pushed all the warning signs away and adhered to the nonsense that surrounded me. Craig was my everything—he was the brother I never got to spend time with, he was the father I longed for, and he was the lover I dreamed of. He became my all, and I had become a victim of my own doing.

Someone special brought about a drastic change in my life. I met Ma B's niece, who had two kids—a son and a daughter. The first time I laid my eyes on that little girl my heart just melted. She was so cute. Her mom wanted her to spend time with Ma B. Ma B was delighted to have her, so I took her home. She was such a sweet little girl, and Ma B wanted her to stay with us if that was okay with me. I started taking her everywhere with me, and everyone just loved her. This became a profound relationship in my life. She became my daughter—a responsibility I was willing to take on.

It was also during this time that some bickering was going on at my job. A few teachers were complaining that I was making more money teaching on the specialist line than they had. They were complaining that it wasn't fair since I hadn't actually gone to a teacher's college. My contract was in jeopardy, and I was about to lose my job. After working there for two years, the principal told me that I was going to be terminated.

I was pained to later find out that my previous job had offered me my old position back, but instead of mailing my re-hire letter they gave it to another teacher who lived in my area. I never received the letter. It was only years after when I reconnected with one of my old coworkers that I found out about the letter during our conversation. He said, "We just thought you didn't want to come back." After our conversation, I called two other teachers who verified his information. They also thought the same thing—that I didn't want to return to the job. I couldn't understand why the other teacher from my area didn't give me the re-hire letter, but I understood one thing— 'Evil.'

My life took a drastic turn. I was unemployed and couldn't land a job. I had interview after interview. My interview at William Field Secondary School went well. However, I wasn't hired. It became a trend. I was repeatedly told, "You will hear from us," but when I did it was never with good news. I was beginning to get frustrated.

The last straw was when I applied for a position at Craig's company. I was well known and liked it there. After the interview, the general manager, Mr. B, sat across from me making small talk. I had already been interviewed by the Personnel Officer, so why did he want to see me? Finally, he got straight to the point. He informed me that it was in his better judgment not to hire me because my rival was being considered. This was the same young lady whom I encountered on my trip from Montego Bay. She had connections—her family members worked there—so they were going to hire her over me. I got up, shook his hand, and left. When I left the office building, everything around me seemed like a blur. "What the hell just happened?"

I didn't discuss the interview with Craig. I didn't ask him why he hadn't informed me that his baby's momma was also seeking employment there. I moved on to seek employment elsewhere.

Sometime later, Craig and I had a nasty breakup that neither of us saw coming. One of his baby mommas wrote me a disturbing letter. We had a big argument. One thing led to another, and we were over. I was so tired of all the women. After our breakup, I used the free time I now had to focus on myself. I took a break from my contraceptive. I tried to find myself by writing more short stories and poems. I felt free—like I was floating in a different world.

I had just been interviewed by the editor of a large newspaper, and I was feeling upbeat. If only my luck would change, so I could get the job. I earnestly prayed for that to happen. While I was waiting to hear back, I tried to examine my current situation pertaining to jobs. I was overqualified for most of the positions I was applying for, or my qualifications were just what they were looking for, so why wasn't I able to gain employment?

Then one evening, I met Jerry McBright when he was on a journalism assignment. We had dinner together. After a few beers, one thing led to another, and I went home with him. I had a one-night stand. He was a free man, and I admired that. At one point, I thought we would really have something going between us, but that part of the relationship never materialized. I was too afraid to get involved with anyone emotionally and too frail to build up any romantic connections. However, our one-night stand led to an unexpectedly deep and profound friendship that lasted for years.

Jerry became the one person I could reason with about anything and everything for hours on end. I still remember our silly laughter over fried chicken and beers. Jerry was a journalist. And in his company, I tried learning the journalistic role of being a writer. He greatly encouraged me to pursue this career.

Almost a year went by since I had spoken to Craig. I still wasn't working, but I was living my life. Every morning, I was thankful for another day. Some days, I would accompany my friend, Big D, to the police garage in Kingston so that he could fix his vehicle. I met Big D while I was attending business school in Port Antonio, Portland. He was stationed there as a police officer. During my two years teaching in Port Antonio, we become very good friends. He would often tease me about his fellow officer, George, who I left hanging for Craig. I think all the officers knew the story about George and me, and how much he wanted to marry me. There were times when I still felt guilty about the way I had ended the relationship.

That Friday, Big D, picked me up. I went along for the ride. After leaving the police garage, we had lunch at one of the Chinese restaurants on Red Hills Road. On our way home, we stopped at 'Stanley's' in Friendship Gap. We went to have a drink and get some fried chicken for my daughter. I was having fun. Big D was well known and respected by everyone. Ma B loved him. They would talk for hours and had formed a special friendship. I continued to enjoy myself, love myself, and be at peace with myself.

Then, one day out of nowhere, Craig sent me a message saying he wanted to see me. At first, I wasn't interested in anything he had to say but I soon agreed to meet with him. Ma B wisely said, "Don't go. Let sleeping dogs lie. You have moved on." But had I? I thought his meeting would be harmless, so I went. I wouldn't let my guard down. Craig came to pick me up, and we went to the nearby Coconut Grove Club. We drank and danced the night away, and it felt so good. That night, I ended up in his bed making sweet love—only he could make me feel fulfilled. The next morning, he looked at me and said, "I think you got pregnant last night." He had a wide grin on his face. The rest of the day I avoided Ma B while I sat reminiscing. There was so much between Craig and me. Did I really want to go back to him? Did I really want to continue waiting for the right man to show up? I still harbored deep feelings for him and still craved his touch, so I knew I wasn't over him. After that night at Craig's, I thought of getting married and just being a good wife to a very deserving man.

CHAPTER NINE

My deep and true reality

I sat in Dr. Jones' office as he confirmed my pregnancy. Dr. Jones asked, "Are you happy?" I nodded. "Yes, I am happy." As I sat on the step of the doctor's office, a million thoughts went through my mind. Craig might not take kindly to this news. I hadn't slept with him for a whole year, and the one time I sleep with him—I get pregnant. What was I thinking? The result of my indiscretion was now a child. I gathered myself together and walked towards the bus stop while a shy smile crept over my face as I thought of the baby.

Later that evening, I saw Craig and told him the news. "Bad timing, my love, bad timing." I knew he wouldn't share the joy I felt. "We have to talk."

"No, I am not having an abortion." I knew he would tell me to do that, so I answered in anticipation of him asking me to.

"I am not saying you should. Let's just talk about this."

I screamed at him, "What is there to talk about? I am pregnant. You don't want any more kids, and I want to keep my baby. There is nothing to talk about."

He looked at me as I walked away. I was a grown woman. I had been through my own hell and survived, so I knew I would survive this alone too. To hell with him! My temper was flaring. How dare he? I calmed myself and took a cab home. This was my reality. With a child on the way, I had an even greater urgency to find meaningful employment.

Two weeks later, I finally got an employment opportunity as an Assistant Communication Director with a great firm. My political friend in high places hooked me up. As I was filling out the paperwork, I told the manager I was three months pregnant. She stopped me right in the middle of my paperwork and told me she couldn't hire me. If only I had kept my big mouth shut. To this day, I still can't figure out why I told her.

After blowing that chance, I was given a job with the Ministry of Agriculture. I was assigned to Castleton Gardens. This was a very beautiful botanical garden with tourist attractions located in the Parish of St. Mary. It was refreshing going to work there even though I just did the payroll and some minimal office duties. It was a job. I didn't complain, and I reported for work every day. I thanked God for this job even though I wasn't earning much. I had time to rest during the pregnancy and basically supervised myself.

One day, Craig came to see me at work. He wanted to apologize for his behavior towards me. He didn't mean for me to abort the baby. He just thought it was bad timing. He looked me all over and complimented me on my weight gain. I was more reserved then and didn't really say much. "Why are you so quiet? I didn't mean to hurt you." I looked at him and saw a faraway look in his eyes. I knew how conflicted he was feeling, and what he must be going through. During our five years together, I had never once missed my period. Now, after being apart for a whole year, it took just one night for us to be discussing a baby.

After months of preparing for the baby's arrival, I was finally in my ninth month. I had been careful by not taking on anything stressful. My mom was in the States then, and I had put my pride aside to ask her if she could send a few things for the baby. She said, "No," and told me off. She reminded me that when she was my age, she had three kids and was able to manage by herself. I cried so much over the contents of the letter because I was so embarrassed. My Aunt Vie, who was in the Bahamas, sent me everything I needed for the baby.

During my pregnancy, my friend, Marvin, reached out to me from across the miles. I met Marvin while traveling to school in Port Antonio. He was a friend of Rita, who used to work on St. Mary's Special. When I was a young girl, he used to tell me tales of his travels. He was a very pleasant person to talk to, and he always treated me with the utmost respect. He was a good and decent man. He worked in the cruise ship industry and was presently in Alaska. I still remember all the postcards he sent me with such uplifting words. Marvin had heard I was pregnant, and immediately wanted to know if he could help in any way. His sobering and reassuring words were enough to uplift my spirit and warm my heart, and he also offered to be the baby's Godfather. In all this, I knew I was going to be okay. The God I served was still with me and would always make a way.

CHAPTER TEN

A new and powerful breakthrough

On August 1st, Emancipation Day, a festive holiday, my beautiful son was born. After hours in labor, he was finally here! My sweet child. Wow! Craig came to look at the baby, and I felt liberated. Our relationship was somewhat distant and strained, but I always put on a brave face and made the most of it.

Although I now had two kids to look after, I was doing a great job at it. My six-year-old daughter welcomed the baby, and so did my cousins, who I had the pleasure of living with in Waterworks, Kingston at the time. My loving and caring cousin, Shelly, helped me out tremendously with caring for the baby. I owe her and her family my profound gratitude for letting me be a part of their lives. While I was living there, I was very happy. I'm also glad I was able to spend some time with the baby before I went back to work.

This was also the beginning of a low point in my life. I remember that my cousin's grandmother had written to her daughter in Chicago and had begged her to send me a pair of shoes because I didn't have any. Although I was upset, embarrassed, and furious to say the least, I knew it was true. All my life I had clothes and shoes to spare, but now I was down to my last pair of flats. I had a few pairs of heels, which were suitable for interviews, but not for job hunting. However, that wasn't on my mind. My focus was to provide for these kids.

My daughter was happy, and my baby was also going to grow up happy with whatever little we had. I made sure they weren't short of anything. God was always with me. In all that I had to overcome; he was still standing with me. Amen.

Now, I needed to focus. I wanted to move my life in a different direction. I needed a shift. I was low on funds, low on self-esteem, and low on energy. I had already hit the ground. How much lower could I get?

Three months after giving birth, I started freelancing with the local newspaper. I would write an article here and there while also cashing in on the love poems I submitted for the Star newspaper every Saturday. It was decent pay, but the money wasn't enough. I needed a salary.

I went back to job hunting, but still, I hit brick walls. I was told repeatedly I was too qualified or that I would hear from them shortly, but all to no avail. Over the weekend, I attended a political conference and saw my friend, who was delighted to see me. He asked me about the baby, and we chatted for a while. He told me to come to his office Monday. When I walked into his office, he was on the phone with Annotto Bay's famous son, who was the general manager of a large government company. I was told to report to the GM the following day—which I did. He was overjoyed to see me. He wasn't a stranger. He went to school with my uncle. We had a good-hearted conversation, and then he asked, "Are you pregnant?" We both burst out laughing. He picked up his phone and called the Personnel Manager. She walked in and looked me over as he introduced me. "Find a suitable position for her."

With that, I walked into her office. As I sat down, she asked me for my resume which I handed to her. "Tell me about yourself," she instructed. I told her my relevant information and that I could start right away. "You'll hear from us," she said. I politely thanked her and then left. As I was leaving, I saw a young lady who I knew. She was waiting to be interviewed too. I stopped to say, "Hi," and asked about her sister. I knew I had the job, so finally, I was feeling relieved. After two weeks had passed, I hadn't been called, so I decided to call the office. I got off the bus at the telephone company on Halfway Tree Road. As I was about to cross the street, I saw the young lady who had been interviewed on the same day as me.

"Why didn't you come to work?" she asked. I was dumbfounded. She continued telling me that she started working last week, and the Personnel Manager had sent out both our letters of employment at the same time. I just stared at her. How could this be? I thanked her and made my way to one of the telephone booths. I called the Personnel Manager. Her secretary answered and asked who was calling. I gave her my name and waited and waited. Finally, Miss Will came on the phone. When I told her I was calling for an update, she replied, "You didn't show up for work, but now you are calling for an update. Don't waste my time," and hung up the phone. I called right back and tried explaining to her that I didn't receive the acceptance letter, but she was having none of what I had to say. Never in my life had anyone talked down to me like this. She went on and on, then again hung up the phone. I burst out crying. Hot tears rolled down my cheeks as I staggered to the bus stop like a drunken sailor. I collapsed on the bench and cried uncontrollably.

A lady walked to the bus stop and saw me crying. "Never mind, my dear, these men are not worth crying over," she said. She assumed I had relationship issues. Through my sniffling, I tried to assure her that wasn't the case. "What's wrong then?" She asked with a puzzled look on her face. I just cried some more, and in between sobbing I told her how I couldn't get a job, despite interviews after interviews. She looked at me with very concerned eyes, and then said seven magical words that changed my life. "I know someone who can help you." God had sent me this earthly angel because he knew I had enough! Yes, at long last, help was on the way.

A new dawn was breaking for me. On a bright and sunny Monday morning, I walked into a building on Knutsford Boulevard that I had always wanted to work in. I had finally gotten a good job. My journey here wasn't easy, but I prevailed by the grace of God. In retrospect, I should've known that my hard luck wouldn't survive my willpower to rise above the ashes. Once again, I was in a nice building with a good job, and as always, some interesting coworkers. I started to live again—to gain control of my life and move in the direction I saw fit.

Five months after I started working, I was given a tremendous opportunity. The Poetry Society of America had informed me that I was a winner in a poetry contest and was invited to attend the grand gala in Anaheim, California at Disney Studios. I was excited, but that was short-lived. I had to get a visa, funding for the trip including plane tickets, hotel accommodations plus fees for the event, and more. The more I thought about not going the more I was convinced I should at least try. My best friend, Caroline, whom I met on the job, encouraged me to at least try to get the visa.

So, on a sunny Tuesday morning in June, I made my way to the U.S. Embassy with all the required documents. I headed to the counter and warmly greeted the Immigration officer. He took my documents, looked them over, congratulated me on winning my prize, and informed me that I should return to pick up my documents later that same day at 3:00 p.m. I was beaming from ear to ear. I could hardly wait to tell Caroline that they took my documents. When I went to pick up my documents, I had been approved for a one-entry visa to the U.S. It was stamped in my passport along with some stipulations, such as, that I could only use the visa for the contest in California.

With the visa in hand, my world of possibilities just opened. I made all the necessary arrangements to go and sought out friends who might be able to help. Everyone in my immediate circle was happy for me. My dear friend in New York told me that I could stay with her sister-in-law while in California. I took out most of my savings for my ticket to Los Angeles plus money to keep me while I was there. I was very excited, and I was already missing my kids and my Ma B.

I got to the Norman Manley International Airport in Kingston and hugged my crying kids. My heart was breaking knowing I was leaving them behind, but I was going to seize this tremendous opportunity given to me through my hard work and my God-given talents. I boarded the plane with a silent prayer to the only true God I served—knowing he was with me.

CHAPTER ELEVEN

My real moment of truth

My flight was on time, and I arrived in LA on a warm Friday night. After I cleared Immigration, I walked over to the baggage claim. As fate would have it, I couldn't find my bags. I looked all over, but my bags were nowhere in sight. An airport employee tried to help me but to no avail. All I had was the suit on my back.

Mrs. G, who was the wife of my Member of Parliament, was on the same flight and came over to inquire. She asked where I was staying, and I gave her the address. The manager at Air Jamaica Airlines had me fill out a form, gave me fifty dollars, and asked me to call the airport in the morning. Mrs. G gave me her contact information and told me not to worry.

I took a cab to the house of my girlfriend's sister-in-law, Susan. The following morning, Susan took me to Kmart. I bought a few pairs of underwear, a bra, a pair of slippers, two dresses, some t-shirts and a pair of Capri pants. All my accessories and my beautiful dress with the matching shoes were in my lost bag.

That same day was the night of the ceremony. As disappointed as I was, I knew I was not going to make it. I was frustrated and angry. What should have been my shining moment was becoming my gloomiest despair. This was my biggest achievement to date. I wanted to bask in its glory; instead, I was like a lost child. What omen could have crossed the miles with me? I wanted to scream, but instead, I went to sleep in the early hours of Sunday morning.

Early that Sunday morning, I called Mrs. G and told her the disappointing news.

As I was about to have breakfast, Susan said we had to talk. She came straight to the point, "I can't have you staying here. I work at night." I just stared at her as she continued. "I can't leave you here with my husband."

I laughed so hard I thought I was going to pass out. "Your husband?"

"I know I said you could stay; however, I don't think it's a good idea now. I booked two nights for you at a motel. I am so sorry."

I was dumbfounded. Her husband? The words just kept playing over and over in my head. I wouldn't ever give her husband a second look. I loved them tall, dark, and handsome. Her husband was none of the three.

As I left her home, I went to hug her very cute kids, and I didn't see her husband. She had checked me into a motel on Sunset Boulevard. She was even "kind" enough to take me there. As I walked into the room, I could smell the Pine-Sol used on the floor. The room looked cheap but clean. It had a double bed, two nightstands, a table-like desk with a chair, and a color television set. The bathroom was also clean. The walls had some stains, but they were hardly visible.

She sat on the bed looking at me. "This was the best I could do."

She opened her pocketbook and I stopped her. "Please, don't. You've done enough."

"Let me at least get you breakfast." We hopped in her car to the nearest McDonald's. I felt like I had just become a charity cause. Back in my motel room, I welcomed the solace. Where do I go from here? Where are my contacts? I called my mom in New York, but she didn't have the money to buy a ticket for me to reach her. I hadn't spoken to my friend in New York since I arrived in California. I didn't anticipate that we would end our friendship but ended it had. I gave Susan a lot of credit for welcoming me into her home even though she suddenly unwelcomed me. She didn't know me from a hole in the wall, yet she was willing to open her home.

I lay on the bed thinking why my stay had gone so terribly wrong when it dawned upon me that I would be going back home tomorrow. The thought frightened me into action. I reached out once again to Mrs. G. I told her where I was, and she said not to worry. She warned me about loitering in front of the motel, and I promised to stay inside. That night, I watched a movie (my first ever in America) and tried to make sense of the situation. In the quietness of the room, it hit me like a thunderbolt.

My one night of indiscretion might have caught up with me and got me in this situation. As my shame washed over me like a power hose washing a car, I shuddered and composed myself. Susan's behavior all made sense now. But what if I was wrong? And how in the world would my friend know I had slept with her father? A few years ago on a Saturday night, two friends and I went bar hopping. The last bar we went to was about to close; however, the bartender decided to serve us even though we were already stoned. The men in the bar were all familiar. My friend's father was vacationing at the time and was buying drinks for everyone in the bar. We all got drunk that night, and I happened to follow him home. I don't know who our mutual friend ended up with, and I never asked. To be honest, I don't think I actually engaged in any sexual activities, but our mutual friend knew I had spent the rest of the night with him. Could she have given me away? Well, I wasn't going to dwell on that. I was just trying to sum up the situation. I rolled over on my side and fell asleep.

The next morning, I woke up with a new resolve. I was going to dismiss all those thoughts from the previous night and let sleeping dogs lie. I called Mrs. G, and she said I could stay with her friend, Maria, in Hollywood for the remainder of my time. I was so relieved to hear such good news. My God had come through for me once again.

The cab driver picked me up at 10:30 a.m. He was a short, pleasant Mexican man. He told me he had moved here ten years ago from his native country, and then eventually he was also able to bring his wife and kids here six years after he had left. He loved LA because of the warm sunshine and fine people. I listened as he spoke so passionately about his job and the satisfaction of being here. I told him I was from Jamaica, and how much I was missing my kids. As he drove up the long driveway, I could see the house amidst the pine trees.

All seemed quiet as I alighted from the car, but just as abruptly, the front door opened, and a lady stood there with open arms to greet me. "You are beautiful," Maria said. I smiled and thanked her. She led me inside her immaculate house. We went upstairs to the bedrooms. The master bedroom and the other four bedrooms all had their own bathrooms. "Pick a room!" I stood in awe looking at the accommodations. I took the room closest to the master bedroom. "I am taking you shopping later." I looked at her, and a big, warm smile lit up my face. "Welcome to Hollywood!"

CHAPTER TWELVE

Happy days are here again!

Maria and I spent the afternoon at the mall. It was wonderful! Not because of all the money she was spending on me, but because she was so much fun. She even tried speaking our Jamaican dialect.

We stopped at one of the restaurants in the mall to grab a bite. It was humid outside, and I welcomed the coolness of the air conditioner on my skin. No sooner had we sat down than I spotted Mrs. G walking in with a handsome lad, who I later learned was her attorney. Maria beckoned her over and extended an invitation to join us. If she was surprised to see us, she didn't betray it. She hugged me and declined the invite. She told Maria she was wrapping up a business matter and promised to stop by the next day. I ordered a bacon cheeseburger deluxe with lettuce and tomato and an ice-cold Heineken. Maria had the same except she ordered some type of white wine. The waitress came with our drinks. I watched as she poured a portion of the Heineken into a glass. I thought, 'I would have drunk it straight from the bottle.'

We finally got home with all the shopping bags. I was exhausted but grateful for the clothes and shoes she just bought me. She even let me get gifts for the kids. Wow! At one point, I wanted to stop her, but Mrs. G had warned me not to insult her by refusing anything she offered to do. Where did this kind, loving, energetic angel come from? It was like she knew me all her life. I am always persuaded to believe that when God is for you then no one can be against you. Through all my misfortunes, pain, emotional turmoil, and trials, God was always standing with me. Only he could have turned this bad experience into this joyous affair. I was now glad I came.

The following day, we went to the airport to check again on my lost bags. The manager, James Morris, had no news for me about my bag, but he gave me a check for $150. I was pleased. I hadn't spent any of the money I took with me from Jamaica. I was well taken care of by my friends. Was this a new wave of luck for me in a foreign land? I tried making sense of it all and was quite pleased that things were turning around for me.

Maria took me to Disneyland in Anaheim. I was excited to see the beautiful landmark, all the rides, and other activities. As I gazed at the hotel where the award ceremony was held, I couldn't help but think of what I might have lost by not attending. However, I had learned not to live my life with regrets. I had accepted that it wasn't meant to be. After leaving Disneyland, she took me to see the Playboy Mansion owned by Hugh Hefner, the Hearst mansion, and the Rock Star Mansion. I just looked at those mansions fully believing at the time that I could only live in one of them if I worked there—maybe as domestic help. I couldn't help remembering my little hut back home in comparison to these mansions. The mansions were so beautiful! You could see the appearance of wealth, and you could feel it too.

The following day, Maria decided to cook. She was making chicken soup. I watched her as she washed three (four-pound whole) chickens with lemon juice, and then put them in the pot with all the vegetables and seasoning. I had never seen anyone cook a whole chicken in a soup—much more three whole chickens. I watched in astonishment. The soup turned out to be very delicious, but I still couldn't fathom why she cooked like she was feeding all of LA. She was overweight, but she was so active. She told me that she had grown up chubby. When she came to California as a little girl, her family had so much food that her mom would feed the homeless people on the street. That really caught my attention because I had never seen so many people lying on the street. Some people had cardboard boxes to shield them from the hard pavement while others had boxes to protect them from the elements. This was homelessness in America! How could this be? With all these rich folks, there are homeless?

My fun times with Maria were slowly coming to an end. I was leaving in two days. After dinner, she called me to her room and asked me if I had considered staying. "You'll have a home right here. My daughter will find you work. I can find someone to marry you asap because I know you have your kids." She must have read something in my expression because she paused. "Think about it." I nodded and left.

I sat in the room analyzing the situation as it presented itself—the chance of a new life in a foreign country with all its glorious opportunities versus my life back home in a third-world country full of crime, poverty, and very little possibility of achievement. However, I put the temptation to stay in California away for good. I couldn't do that to my kids. I knew Ma B would take care of them, but it wasn't fair to her. She had already raised me. Besides, what if something happened to her? Would I be able to go home then? "Oh, no," I said aloud. I just couldn't do that.

On my last day in California, we went to the Hollywood Walk of Fame on Hollywood Boulevard. On the brochure, it's described as "the street where Hollywood stars are immortalized with bronze star plaques, embedded in pink and charcoal terrazzo squares." I saw the names of so many stars! Maria asked me who was my favorite star. I just said the first name that came to mind. "Joan Collins." In retrospect, I could have said any of the lead characters from the hit drama, "Dynasty." However, Joan Collins was the badass in the show.

My last day was very memorable. Maria got me more clothes. I got souvenirs for my coworkers. I took another look at this phenomenal construction called 'the freeway.' I loved the freeway with its traffic going in all directions. It was so amazing. When we got home, I unpacked the new stuff I just got. I couldn't help but think of all the fun I had, and how I wished my kids were there with me. I missed them so much. For the rest of the afternoon, we sat by the pool entertaining her two friends along with their four kids. They all loved Mexico and talked about the rich culture of food and drinks—tacos and Tequila. I could hardly wait to get on board with the Tequila. I liked the sound as it rolled off the tongue—Tequila. Even then, Mexico was famous for its resorts in Cancun and its white-sand beaches.

When night fell, the conversation turned to drugs, cartels, and coyotes from Colombia. The tales they talked about had me cracking up with laughter. At one point, I thought the tequila had gotten to my head. There was so much fun happening. Maria's daughter, Ramona, and husband stopped by to bid me farewell. They were so polite and likable.

As Ramona raised her glass, everyone followed. "Salute!"

CHAPTER THIRTEEN

Recovering from the aftermath of a storm

I arrived in Jamaica to death and destruction. While I was away, Hurricane Gilbert struck the island. The devastation was everywhere. The storm was packing winds of 125 mph. It made landfall as a category three storm, and just blanketed the entire island.

As I drove through my hometown, the ruins were evident. Mangled zincs, broken furniture, roofless houses, and metals were a sight to behold for miles. My heart sank. The little house I lived in couldn't have withstood a storm of this magnitude. I braced myself for the worst as I couldn't shake the feeling of uncontrollable loss. As I got out of the car, I could see the house was still standing but a great portion of the roofing was gone along with the front side. Someone had gathered the zincs and boards and placed them in a bundle on the side of the house. My neighbor's house was also there. I whispered a prayer to God thanking him for his mercy. The driver helped me with my suitcases. My kids came running out. I hugged them as I started to cry.

"It's ok," I told them. "Mommy is here now." They wouldn't let me go. I couldn't help but wonder how traumatic it must have been for them while the storm raged with its howling winds and rain. I was relieved to see my grandparents and kids, especially my grandfather. He was so happy to see me.

Later that evening, I unpacked one of the suitcases and gave him the clothes I had bought him. I bought him suitable church clothes—a pair of pants, a white shirt, a tie, a pair of black shoes even some underwear. Ma B was delighted with her two dresses, a pair of shoes, a pair of slippers, a pocketbook, and underwear as well. The kids were delighted to see their gifts. I was just trying to lighten the moment for them. Then, my son said something that had me crying all over again. "Mommy, I thought you weren't coming back." I just stared at them while I sobbed. I could never do that to them—ever. That night we hardly slept as the rest of the roof threatened to collapse.

Early next morning, the workman, Mr. D, came by and accessed the damages to the house with us. He made a list of the materials he would need to carry out the repairs. For the next two days, nothing happened as most of the business places were still closed. I waited for Mr. D to send word as he had informed me earlier that Haffizulla's hardware store was about to reopen. I had the money I took with me to LA plus the money Air Jamaica had given me for my lost bag. After the foreign exchange conversion, I was able to buy the items needed for the repairs. I bought zincs, boards, paint and everything else we needed.

The following week, we started the repairs. I told Mr. D to hire someone to help him as I needed these repairs done expeditiously. We slept at night looking into the sky, and I didn't want that to continue. Thankfully, Friday afternoon, I had a brand-new, freshly painted house. I was happy everything was completed.

I felt so bad for the people who had to wait for government aid to help them repair their homes. I gave the leftover materials to my neighbor. Mr. D wanted them, but I told him no. He might have thought that he could have me buy surplus materials and then take whatever was leftover, but I knew all the ways they tried to use their brains to pull a fast one on you. Believe me, I wasn't the one to try that with—after all he was not working for free. God had worked everything in my favor. I paid Mr. D and gave him a few dollars extra so that he could tip the other two men who helped him. I was very pleased with the results.

The following Thursday, I returned to work as electricity had returned to Kingston. Everyone in my unit was happy to see me. The tale of Hurricane Gilbert dominated the morning conversations as we all shared our personal stories. My boss welcomed me back, and he was genuinely happy to see me. I gave my coworkers their souvenirs and then settled down to work. I was away for almost six weeks, and the files on my desk looked like a mountain. I quickly looked through my messages and began to work. After work, I was going to spend the night with my best friend, Caroline. We had so much to talk about. I had really missed her and couldn't wait to tell her about my adventures in the "Golden State."

That night, we settled down after dinner. We talked about the aftermath of the storm, how most of the island was still without power, and how the death toll kept rising. I had bought a bottle of tequila with me for Caroline to try. I even had the shot glasses for it. I explained to her how it should be consumed. I poured out two shots and gave her one. I watched her face as she swallowed down the liquor. Her face said it all. She didn't like it and resorted to her Stone Ginger wine while I took another shot of Tequila. I loved the liquor. I had come to acquire the taste of one of Mexico's finest distilled spirits.

At work, the job was more tedious. More and more customers were coming in to report the damages to their homes from the storm. My phone rang. It was my son's father, Craig. We chatted for a while, and then I told him I had to go. As I hung up the phone, a deep sadness crept up on me. I missed him so much. However, we had moved on. But had we? My heart still ached from the pain of the separation. I shook the memories off and continued with my work.

I was looking forward to the weekend. I had gotten new mattresses for the kids' beds, and I would finally be able to spend some quality time with them. After breakfast on Saturday, I took them and Ma B with me to the furniture store. We picked up the mattresses and a new chair for my grandfather. Then, we got groceries from the Supermarket and headed home. On Sunday, we went to church to lift our nation up in prayer and to thank God for his favors.

A couple weeks had passed, and life was returning to normal. Some places were still without power, but things were looking up again. Caroline and four other coworkers were planning to go to Miami to shop for Christmas, and she wanted me to come along. She encouraged me to pay another visit to the U.S. Embassy to apply for another visa. My one entry visa had long expired; I decided to give it a shot.

It was a beautiful morning in November when I walked into the embassy with a new job letter and bank statement. A little girl stood in line with her parents. I smiled at her, but she just tugged on her mother's dress. They called, "Next," and they stepped up to the counter. I waited. When I got to the counter, I could not believe my eyes. It was the same interviewer I had prior. I flashed my signature smile and again warmly greeted him. This was my lucky day. He actually remembered me and asked about the convention and how I liked LA. We were just having a conversation—not an interview. He took my documents and told me to return at 3:00 p.m. Everyone standing in line looked at me like I was some sort of celebrity. Some people gave me the evil eyes while others just looked away as I made my way back from the counter smiling.

At work, I told Caroline what had happened. She was so thrilled even though she had no knowledge I was going that day. I could hardly wait to see what type of multiple-entry visa I would have stamped on my passport. As I sat in the waiting area to be called to get my passport back, I couldn't help but wonder how my God could love me so much. I got my passport and walked outside where a small group of women had gathered to compare each other's stamps. I had put my passport into my pocket and headed for work.

At work, I walked into the ladies' restroom and locked myself in the stall. I opened my passport. I could hardly contain my glee. I had an indefinite multiple-entry visa stamped on my passport. I hurried outside to find Caroline. We hugged. My heart felt like it was bursting with joy. I had been vindicated in every possible way. Now, I had more opportunities opening to me and more choices. However, how I used those choices were entirely up to me. The Christmas shopping was on! I started taking orders at work from my coworkers. In doing so, I was taking the hassle out of peddling for their gifts. Shoes were more lucrative, so everyone wanted a pair of shoes that matched our uniforms. I was excited about going and was receptive to making extra money. For the next couple of weeks, I worked overtime by going into the office on Saturdays and Sundays. I took the kids with me one Sunday, and they loved it. My boss was very accommodating, and I was grateful. My life had taken a new turn, and I was going to let God steer the wheel.

CHAPTER FOURTEEN

My travelling took on a new meaning

Air Jamaica flight, 0063, landed in Miami at 7:48 p.m. on a warm Friday night in December. The night sky was lit up by the stars as the drizzling rain gave way to lovely weather. We arrived at the Everglades Hotel in downtown Miami, and the atmosphere was inviting. The courteous and friendly staff were superb in getting us checked in. The chandeliers hanging in the lobby areas were magnificent and gave off a flow of luxurious vibes. We hurried up to our suites and lay across the two queen-size beds.

Our supervisor left with a friend, so Caroline and I decided to hang out at the bar in the hotel drinking Heineken beers and margaritas. A few guys came up to us offering to buy us drinks; however, we politely declined. At one point, a guy asked for my number. When I told him no, he left me his. I wasn't living there, and I didn't want to be bothered.

After breakfast, we hit the road. We went shopping and tried to find bargains that would yield a return on our money. We barely had time to grab a bite during the day. Later that night, Caroline and I decided to check out one of the nightclubs for a few hours. We had a ball! On Sunday morning, we went to the flea markets and got very good bargains. We hardly had time to get back to the hotel and finish packing before heading out to the airport to catch our flight back home. What a weekend it had been!

I asked the JUTA taxi driver, who took me home, to wait while I got dressed for work. At the office, everyone wanted to know if I got their orders—which I did. However, they would have to wait until the next day to get their merchandise. By Thursday afternoon, everything was gone. All I had to do now was sit back, and watch the money roll in. I wasn't trying to undercut anyone, But I sold my goods at reasonable prices.

Christmas came and went. And with the New Year approaching, it was time to make new resolutions. I had only one—to continue walking in God's grace. I had a plan for my life going forward, but could I execute it?

It was the first Saturday in January, and I had a meeting in Kingston with this guy. I was told that he could advance my career. I wanted to become a serious writer and was working towards that achievement. I didn't know how serious he was because when I met him, he seemed more preoccupied with being untrue to his own vows than helping someone professionally; however, I had to try. During the meeting, I realized it was a complete waste of time. I quickly dismissed all the personal questions he tried asking me. I thanked him and left. I was just going to continue contributing articles to the local newspapers and biding my time.

Life had a way of taking me all over the place with my emotions, but I had been in the company of men like him before. I was prepared or so I thought. I returned home that night feeling drained. I was about to go to the club, the famous Coconut Grove, which stood in the middle of town, but quickly changed my mind. I'm glad I didn't go. It was a restful weekend, and I got to spend quality time with my family.

Mr. Smooth Talk was the nickname I gave the guy I had the meeting with two weeks ago. He had called me every day since the meeting. A week went by, and he called again. He wanted to take me out for lunch, and I had accepted. We settled down to eat, and I ordered a Heineken beer. The menu was loaded with so many dishes to choose from. I decided to have the stewed pork—thinking he would be turned off as some men in Jamaica didn't eat pork but that didn't seem to bother him. He ordered water and the steak with rice and peas. I knew he was coming onto me, but I wasn't interested.

As time passed, I tried so hard, yet I couldn't keep my emotions in check. One night, a guy I knew offered me a ride home. We stopped by the Coconut Grove Club. He ordered fried chicken to go along with our drinks. We sat there listening to some good solid music like "Didn't We Almost Have It All" followed by "Where Do Broken Hearts Go?" Out of nowhere, I just started crying. I thought my heart would burst open. Poor guy. People at the bar walked over to our table to find out why I was crying. He had no clue and hurriedly took me home. I apologized to him, but that wasn't enough. He never gave me a ride again. In retrospect, I shouldn't have put him in that situation and should have declined his offer.

After a few months, I decided to date Mr. Smooth Talk. The sex was good, but I had to teach him a lot in the bedroom. He was well endowed but didn't know how to use it. I always had to be the lead in the bedroom. I dated him for almost a year before the relationship ended. There were times when I missed the sex, but I still didn't meet up with him. He was a very decent person and very kind, but I wasn't emotionally ready for any kind of serious relationship that included intimacy.

I was so broken inside that pretending on the outside was getting more difficult for me. I thought of going to counseling but decided against it. I didn't want to relive old trauma to understand my present situation, and that's what counselors do. However, I had to move past all this. I never knew you could miss someone so deeply that your whole world seemed to be crumbling before your eyes.

I decided to visit my mom and sister in New York for the Easter holiday. Caroline was arranging a trip to Curacao, but I didn't want to go. She asked me to come with her to Gitmo in Guantanamo Bay. Her brother and cousin worked on a boat there. I said no to that trip too. Old demons threatened to return. So instead, I travelled to New York. I was super happy to see my mom and sister. I could see the outer appearance changes in my mom. She was now a Christian and serving the Lord. My sister was also active in the same church. I could hardly wait for Sunday to come so that I could see my sister pouring out her soul in the songs. On Saturday, they took me to Manhattan. I rode the tour bus through the city as the guide pointed out all the landmark places. I shopped at Macy's to get a dress and a pair of shoes for church. My sister could put a hat together in no time, and she promised to make me one that night. On Sunday, everything was glorious. The preacher delivered a touching message. I was so moved that when they gave the 'Altar Call,' I went up for prayers.

My mom had taken Wednesday off so that we were able to see my grandaunt and cousin in Jamaica, Queens—in Laurelton Gardens to be exact. We arrived at my cousin's house first and had refreshments. She gave me a tour of her lovely home, then she started asking me personal questions about my life—things she had no business asking me about. I was so disgusted with her attitude that I was happy to leave for my aunt's house. She too had a lovely home. She asked about her brother, my grandfather, who she hadn't spoken to in years. After she decided to share dinner with us, my sister pulled me away and told me to be careful with the food. I couldn't understand what she meant. Was she trying to poison me? After reading my concerned expression, my sister clarified. "Oh, no, she loves to serve stale food." Suddenly, I was no longer hungry.

The next day we went to Conway department store and Macys at 34th street in Manhattan. My sister must have seen me with all my U.S. dollars and thought I was well off when nothing could've been further from the truth.

My week passed too quickly, and soon it was time to leave. I hugged my mom and sister and left for the airport. I really enjoyed the time I spent with them. Yet, I still didn't accomplish my real goal which was to confide in my mother and tell her the secret I had been carrying all these years. I just couldn't do it.

On the flight back home, I was deep in thought. My relationship with Craig needed closure, but I had buried all those painful events—never wanting them to resurface again. After I had my son, I went back to sleeping with Craig. I even got pregnant again. That time without any hesitation I got an abortion and quickly got back on the pill. The abortion ripped into my soul, but it was the right thing for me. I already had two kids. How could I manage financially with another? I put the guilt and the shame away and continued to be with him.

After all, he had put me through, I still hadn't had enough. It's strange how older folks can always see the inevitable. One night, Ma B told me when she heard me crying in the darkness of my room that she knew I hadn't had enough just yet, and when I had enough—I would run. I kept going back to him. No matter how embarrassing the situation. I would look past it and fall right back in his arms. I thought seeing him with someone else after travelling over sixty miles to visit him would do it, but that didn't stop me. Neither did the time I was with him when another woman pounded on the door of his house. In my head, he made me feel so special. And I believed I was also special to him. But after all the emotional turmoil, I met my last straw.

I was living with my cousin in Waterworks in Constant Spring. During this time, I would go hang out with Craig after his shift depending on his assignments. On a Friday afternoon, I saw him off to Montego Bay. I was heading back home when one of his coworkers, who I liked, asked me to have a drink with him. We stopped by a bar on Barry Street in western Kingston close to the Railway Headquarters. He asked me what the state of the relationship between Craig and me was. I told him everything was cool between us. He made a painful face and turned away. I knew something was terribly wrong.

"What is it?"

"I love you like a sister, and I hate to see him making a fool of you."

My initial thought was that Craig had gotten another woman pregnant, or worst yet, he was about to settle down with someone else. I braced myself for the bad news. In retrospect, it's funny how none of his coworkers had ever approached me before to rat him out.

He got straight to the point. "Whenever you come to meet him after his shift, do you two go home together?"

"No, he lives in May Pen and is always trying to get home." He was silent for a few moments as I continued. "Craig has been saying recently how difficult it has become for him to get home after signing off from those late-night assignments."

He looked at me, shook his head, and took a sip of the rum and coke he was drinking. He then said, "Well, his baby's mother lives in Portmore, and that's where he goes."

"I didn't know that. Thanks for telling me."

And with that, I was out of the bar like a fire racing through an old building. I could hardly contain myself. My heart was pounding like I was getting a heart attack. I cried all the way home, and then I cried all through the night. I guess everyone was laughing at me.

Suddenly, everything made sense. Whenever I would go see him on his job, she would always be there. She would always find something to come see him about. I often wondered why she couldn't just wait until I had left. I had just dismissed it as her trying to get to my head. Now, I see her message was that she was in charge. Oh, what a fool I had been all this time.

That Sunday evening, I got ready and went to meet him as usual. He seemed genuinely happy to see me, and even brought me back something from Montego Bay. I cringed as he held me in his arms to kiss me, but I was ready to do what I couldn't do for all those years. We came to the bus stop. I told him to board his bus first. He looked at me with puzzled eyes. Then, I just gave him a hug and walked away.

That was how it all ended. I stopped taking his calls. I stopped going to see him. Whenever he came to see me, I would hide. I wouldn't answer any of his messages. We had nothing to discuss, and so, there was no finale. It took him a while to realize I was gone for good this time.

The touchdown of the plane jerked me back to reality. As the passengers clapped, I was still in a daze. He haunted my dreams. I knew something would have to give. I just couldn't go on like this—not anymore. 'God, where are you?'

CHAPTER FIFTEEN

A different path from what I envisioned

Manor Park Plaza across from Constant Spring Road in Kingston was where workers who lived along the Junction Road and beyond would gather in the evenings to catch the public transportation home. Even tourists, who came to the city for the purpose of shopping, would come to that spot to get a ride home. It was frequently referred to as "the Hitchhiker's Corner." Most people failed to understand that most of those hitchhikers were hard-working people—like me—just trying to get home.

I had decided to travel to Annotto Bay to spend the night with my kids. I stayed in Kingston because of my job; however, I tried to be with them at least two nights a week plus the weekends. I left work early. I got off the bus and walked toward the gas station. I headed for my favorite spot—the little bridge that stood over the gully below. I was lost in thought when I heard a horn. I looked up and a Benz motorcar had stopped at my feet. The man driving asked, "Where are you going?" I looked at him. He was well dressed and flashed me a smile that showed off his gold tooth. Before I could answer him, he was stretching over to open the door for me.

We talked light-heartedly. He told me that he used to live in the States but came home because the U.S. government was out to get him. I smiled to myself. I knew before he even uttered a word that it was drug related. He told me he bought Eli Matalon's house in the hills of St. Andrew. At that time, Eli Matalon was the wealthiest man in Jamaica. He was a member of the People's National Party and was one of Jamaica's beloved sons. By then, he had left public office and migrated to Miami. For this man to have bought his house spoke volumes.

I arrived at my destination and thanked him. He gave me his number, and in return, I gave him my job number. When I came out of the car, my kids came to greet me. They were always looking out for me whether they knew I was coming home or not. He asked me where their father was, and I thought that was none of his business to ask.

He drove off while I listened to my son tell me something Ma B did. These kids were my pride and joy. We walked to the nearby store by the beachfront, and I got them refreshments. When we got home, my daughter had completed her homework, so I had to check to see that her work was correct.

At work the next day, my phone rang, and it was "Boss Man." I later learned his workers called him "The Boss."

"What's up, pretty girl? You want to go for lunch?"

"Thanks, but I will have to take a rain check. I have a lot of work." I quickly ended the conversation and began to concentrate on the mortgage account I was going over. Since I came back from New York, I was a little calmer and more like my usual self. I put almost all of my time into my work. "The Boss" or Randy would call daily to check up on me, but he never crossed the line of being rude. He always politely asked, "When are we having lunch?"

The following Thursday, I was having a headache and I needed a break. The mortgage accounts I had been working on with my coworker, Faithy, weren't balancing. I had called it quits when the phone rang. It was Randy's daily call. We chatted for a while, and then he asked the magic question, "When are we having lunch?"

"Today," I replied. He was surprised but arranged to pick me up at 12:30 p.m. We went to a Chinese restaurant on Red Hills Road. I ordered Chicken Chop Suey and he ordered Shrimp Lo Mein. Maybe it was the atmosphere in the restaurant, but I felt completely at ease in his company. I brought back lunch for Faithy. I was late getting back to the office, but no one noticed.

Over the next several weeks, I regularly saw Randy. Sometimes, I just drove around with him in the evenings while he monitored the buses he owned. He would pick me up at work, and then drive up to the Halfway Tree neighborhood to watch over his workers. They would address us as "Boss and Boss Lady." He was so cool. He took me to his office to meet the lady who did the accounting for his business. She took one look at me and turned her head away. That was not good. The lady, Miss Pam, didn't like me one bit. I was ready to leave, but he was there on business. She showed him the sum of money with checks and cash included that she would be taking to the bank in the morning. She told him, "Today wasn't a good one." I thought, 'Of course not, you met me, you bitch.'

After his business was done, he gathered his things. "Let's go have a drink?" We drove up to Piper's Lounge on Constant Spring Road. They treated us like Royalty. I was enjoying all the attention. I thought to myself, 'Yes, this was the distraction I needed.' Randy and I talked about New York and Miami. He hadn't been to California.

Then he asked me, "How come you're single?"

"I'm not."

"Well, yes, you have me now." I bust out laughing. He continued, "Well, you had me from the first day I saw you."

"Really? Well, that's not how you ask someone to be with you."

"Think about it."

I liked him, but only because he served as a distraction. Was this dangerous? This man, Randy, wanted me to be hopelessly devoted to him; however, I couldn't do that. Even though I thought I was heading in the wrong direction, I decided to continue heading down this path.

At work, everyone knew I had a rich man. He took me—along with Caroline, Faithy, and two other co-workers—out for lunch. He shot the breeze and told them not to pay on any of his buses. They all liked him. Now, I found myself constantly in his company. What the hell was wrong with me?

One afternoon, he took my darling cousin and me to his house in Cherry Gardens in the hills of St. Andrew. The beautiful gardens, the well-kept lawn, and the gorgeous swimming pool were a sight to behold. The house was a mansion. I took a Heineken from the refrigerator and drank it straight from the bottle. My cousin had wine.

I asked my cousin, "Where is the 'Lady of the House'?" My cousin just rolled her eyes at me. I looked at him, "Where is she?"

"There is no her," he replied.

My cousin and I just laughed. We enjoyed a lovely afternoon in his company sitting by the pool and taking in the atmosphere.

When we got back, my cousin finally asked me what my plans were regarding Randy. I told her the truth. I was just living in the moment. She looked at me and shook her head. "Don't you think that's dangerous?" I took some time to think over what my cousin had just asked; however, I just shrugged it off. I had been living on the edge for a long time. How much more dangerous could this be?

That following weekend, Caroline, I, and two others were going to Miami. He was acting like he called the shots—like he was trying to get me to stay. However, it didn't matter to me. We left for Miami the following evening.

In Miami, I sat at the bar in the Everglades Hotel assessing my life. The last few months had been a whirlwind for me. Miami was a good reprieve, but not a long-term solution. I felt like one day I would break under the weight I was carrying. I was far from acting normal. I needed to get myself into a counseling program, but every time I thought of telling this secret aloud again, I was boxed further in. I had been wavering in my belief lately. I just needed to draw closer to God. But tonight, I would let it all hang out...

CHAPTER SIXTEEN

My cousins, my friends

The weekend in Miami was great. On Saturday morning, we shopped downtown. And on Saturday night, we painted the town red. And then on Sunday, we headed to the flea market. I came back home, and nothing had changed. I just had a little extra money.

Everything was looking rosy for me. I was earning a good salary from working overtime and from selling a lot of our merchandise. But the pain of my past still lingered.

As my cousin, Buck, once said, "Sometimes, the gravity of one's pain is camouflaged by a simple smile, and that cheerful performance is just an act of fear of the unknown." That was me—straight from a textbook. I knew I needed help, but I wasn't going to embrace the unknown.

When Monday morning came around, I returned to work feeling drained from all the activities of the weekend. I should have taken the day off, but I decided against it. I brought most of the order requests to work and distributed them to my coworkers. Now, I needed to focus, and try not to spend so much time in Randy's company. I had yet to see the dark side of him. He was always calm, cool, and collected. I couldn't do anything to get on his nerves. I had started going home more often in the evenings just to break the hold he was trying to place on me.

My cousin, Paul, was his friend, and they got along fine. I asked Randy to get a Canadian visa for Paul. I asked him because Randy's neighbor was the Canadian High Commissioner. Cousin Paul was excited about the prospects of getting a visitor visa to Canada because he was planning on not coming back. His goal was to stay there and make something of his life. Some evenings, after taking me home, Randy and Cousin Paul would go sit by the beach and smoke marijuana. You could smell the strong scent of the weed from a mile away.

By then, I was planning on taking my second trip to Canada and wanted my cousin Paul to come along with me. Randy didn't want to get him the visa. One night, I asked him, "Why don't you want to get my cousin Paul a visa?" He just changed the subject. I knew then that it wasn't going to happen for my cousin. In retrospect, Randy knew my cousin wouldn't use the visa in good faith or return after it had expired. He also probably didn't want to disappoint the High Commissioner.

The following week, I left for Canada to spend ten days there. It was a more relaxing trip. I wasn't expecting to do any heavy shopping. I was only going to buy a few items for my family. My daughter was growing gracefully, and my son was trying to catch up to her. I loved those kids. They were my world. I wanted them to get a good education, and then be contributing members of society. I couldn't see myself in them at their ages. I was a child fighting to live and fighting to be, and I'm glad my kids were better. These kids were healthy, strong, and had a mother who tried to give them everything. I needed a good foundation for them. At night, I often tried to figure out how to incorporate their well-being into my grand plan for the future.

I loved Canada. It was so clean, and a lovely country. It contained beautiful landmarks, such as the CN Tower in Toronto and the Parliament Hill building in Ontario. I was in awe looking at the Parliament Hill building in the capital, Ottawa. The building consisted of all the lawmakers' offices and chambers. My cousins and I had lunch at a little restaurant, which stood out from the rest, near the Heart & Crown Irish Pub. The barbecue chicken and ribs were mouth-wateringly good along with the fries, the mac & cheese, and the cold Budweiser beer. My two cousins had the same except they had Coors Light beers.

Back at my cousin's house, we drank more beer, ate buffalo wings, and just shot the breeze. I was having the time of my life. A few days later, we went to Caribana. Caribana, a festival celebrating Caribbean heritage, is one of North America's largest celebrations, and people come from all over to dance in the streets and just have nonstop fun. I met a guy from Quebec, which is located in the Eastern Province of Canada, and he invited me to their winter festival. I told him I would go in any other season but winter. He said winter was what made the festival fun.

Over the weekend, we went to the beautiful city of Montreal. Then, we drove to Niagara Falls. The falls have two sides: one in New York, and one in Canada. We went to Casino Niagara. I won a couple of dollars and played it all back. We stayed at a hotel for the night. The following morning, we drove back to Toronto. The cool breeze along with the Monday morning blues was in a full circle. Have you ever wondered where everyone is going on a Monday morning? The overhead signs cautioned major congestion ahead. We chose the next exit and detoured.

A little restaurant stood out to us, so we decided to have breakfast and kill time until the traffic got lighter. The aroma of bacon filled the air as we were seated at the table closest to the kitchen. We scanned the menu and placed our orders. The Columbian coffee tasted really good and was the ideal choice along with the bacon, eggs, and whole-wheat toast I ordered. I looked through the morning newspaper that was placed at the entrance of the restaurant. No one in my party was interested in the newspaper. I went looking for the gossip column and was disappointed when I didn't find one. It would seem that no one gossiped in Canada.

It was 11:00 a.m. when we left the place. All the heavy morning traffic was gone, and it was a smooth ride home. I only had one more day until my vacation would be over, so we planned to see a movie later that evening.

I had a fantastic time, but as always, I was longing to see my kids and Ma B and Grandpa. At the Toronto International Airport, I bade my cousins goodbye and boarded the plane to Jamaica. I never lost sight of God as I thanked him for all his Grace and Mercy.

CHAPTER SEVENTEEN

My past demons threaten to return

Randy picked me up from the airport in Kingston. The flight was delayed for 45 minutes, but all was well. He talked about how he missed me, and how I needed to spend more time with him. All I talked about was the wonderful time I had in Canada with my cousins, and how I was looking forward to returning to work.

At work, my coworkers were overwhelmed with caseloads, and so they were relieved to see me. I started working on the backlogs right away.

The weekend after my return, I was taking the kids to Passley Garden in Hope Bay, Portland. I needed to spend quality time with them. My son, JJ, was asking me a lot of questions, and I knew that I needed to spend a whole week with them. Coming home in the evenings was not enough.

During my lunchtime, I reflected on and summed up my life. It was pretty good. I had come a long way. Even though I had always believed that my life was already paved out for me, I needed to follow my own path to great wealth and success. I also knew that my struggles were not over. With me, there would always be something. One thing would be off, another thing would be on, and true happiness would always elude me.

I clung to the words in Psalm 27 (KJV) and Psalm 91 (KJV) and reflected on the magnitude of David's problems. He showed such remarkable strength, and I knew then that I must draw my strength from the words. It was the words that God had intended us to live by. We should draw from the scriptures as we adhere to our everyday lives.

Craig came to my office to see me. My first thought was that he needed my help. I sat at my desk and stared him down. He looked as handsome as ever with that wicked smile showing his lily-white teeth. I finished the account I was working on and turned my attention to him.

"Can we do lunch?" he asked.

"Yes,'" I replied.

I grabbed my pocketbook. We headed for the door and walked to the corner where the lunch crowd was moderate. I glanced at my watch to make sure it was 1:08 p.m. The waitress seated us, and I ordered an iced tea while he ordered a Red Stripe beer. The humidity was somewhat uncomfortable. I heard someone from the adjacent table request for the air conditioner to be turned up.

Craig seemed relatively quiet.

"What's up?" I asked.

"I want you back."

My heart cried out, "Hallelujah," but still I said, "No, Craig, it's too late for that now."

"Just think about it."

There was nothing to think about. I knew in my heart I still loved and missed him tremendously, but I also knew we were over.

He changed subjects. "So, how was Canada?"

"Are you keeping tabs on me now? How did you know I was there?"

"My coworker was on the return flight with you."

"It was fun. I had a lot of fun."

Our food came, and we ate in silence. This wasn't good. Something was amiss. I was afraid to ask him because I wanted to avoid this getting back together notion he had. He quickly changed his mood and became very talkative. He talked about the state of the country and where the

Labor Party was heading. I listened while he vents about the party he supported and was not happy with their policies now. I always admired his passion for politics. He paid, and then we left.

As I walked him to his car and thanked him for lunch, he looked at me, smiled, then said, "I still love you." I slowly walked away as my eyes became watery with tears. The truth was I still loved him too, but our time was over. I arrived back at the office and started working. I was determined not to stay late. I was going home after work. Craig was bad for me. He just stirred up old familiar feelings within me, and my body started craving his touch again. I needed to stay away from his presence. After all this time, I still wasn't completely over him.

That night, I fought back tears as I rested in bed thinking about what might have been between us. I earnestly prayed for God to take away the feelings I still had for Craig. I also prayed for my life to take on a new meaning and travel in a new direction. If I continued to ride on this emotional roller coaster, I would only lead myself down a destructive path. What was it that continued to perplex my soul and haunt me so much?

Even though, I found myself pulling away from Randy and his unforeseen danger. I was still sinking deeper and deeper into this dark abyss of irreversible ruin. My soul was so troubled with bottled-up emotions that putting them in perspective was almost impossible. It was like being in a whirlwind. These feelings toppled each other over and over in an endless circle of despair and loss. I needed to find my way again. But was I ever at peace? I thought of going back to the Church and rededicating my life to God. He was the only one keeping me from losing my sanity even though I had already lost myself.

CHAPTER EIGHTEEN

A calm voice of reasoning

I was very uneasy not knowing where I would find myself next. Right now, I wasn't in a good place.

The kids were striving, and I asked God for protection over them every day. I looked at Ma B and she was still going strong, but Grandpa's health was failing. A few times JJ had found him passed out in the backyard, and we had to revive him.

The next day after we found him passed out again, I requested the day off and took him to a private doctor, so that the doctor could run some tests. The doctor diagnosed it as typical old age. However, if I wanted a definite answer, I would have to return later for the test results.

When we returned home, it was only Ma B there. The kids were at school, and so it was just the three of us. I had bought lunch for us and pastries for the kids while grandpa and I were in town. As we sat by the side of the house, I realized I hadn't been spending any quality time with them, so I decided to spend the following day with them too.

I washed Ma B's hair and realized that I could count her grey strands. They were getting up in age.

Ma B was the one I leaned on and confided in—no matter what my situations were. She could sense something was off with me. As we walked to the nearby store, she asked what was bothering me so much.

"I heard you crying last night."

I wasn't surprised when she told me. I took a minute to compose myself, and then I replied, "I cry all the time, Ma B."

"No, you shouldn't. Look at how far you've come. You travel the world. Look at your achievements. Be happy."

"I am happy."

"No, you're not. You need to let sleeping dogs lie, and move on," she argued.

"I am trying," I reassured her.

She just looked at me. We walked further to the shore and sat on one of the nearby benches.

"It's like there is always something," I told her.

"But you need to continue fighting, my child."

"I am tired." I told her about going to lunch with Craig, and how being in his presence opened old wounds.

"You need to free yourself from those demons, once and for all," she advised.

"I am trying, but I don't know how to. Believe me, I am trying."

"Why don't you see someone who could counsel you?"

I looked into her concern-filled eyes, and stated, "You are my Counselor."

"This is too big for me. You need a professional," she insisted.

I always knew I needed to go see a counselor, but I was too afraid to give in and go. I dreaded all the questions they would ask. I dreaded all the shame and all the guilt I would have to relive. I was strong enough for anything except for counseling. She saw the terrified look on my face and held me in a warm embrace. I felt like a small child again caught up in a welcoming cuddle.

We got back home, and I started preparing dinner. Soon, my son was home and was so happy to see me. He just kissed me again and again. My daughter had stayed back at school for extra lessons. That evening, as the five of us, were seated at the dinner table, I realized that my family was everything. We had a lovely dinner and then settled down to play card games with my cousin Paul.

As the kids and the elders retired for bed, Paul and I walked to the little shop by the beach. We bought a six-pack of Heineken beers and sat on the benches by the sea. We watched the waves just like I used to as a child growing up here. The fresh seawater splashed on my toes. Paul built a spliff and lit up. It's funny how I grew up here in the weed den, and yet I had never smoked it. He asked me about Randy, and the Canadian visa he had promised to give him. I couldn't tell him that it was not forthcoming, so I told him that Randy was still working on it. I wished I had the tools to get my cousin out of here. We chatted and drank beers while the cool night air and the strong scent of weed fumigated the surroundings. It was after midnight when I got home.

The next day, I took Ma B to Port Maria to look over some paperwork. After that, I took her to a restaurant where we sat and had lunch together. Then, we walked to a clothing store where I told her to get whatever she wanted. She looked around at the dresses, and then she picked out this beautifully styled outfit. We went to the dressing room, and it perfectly fit her. At the next store, she bought two pieces of materials to sew dresses. My grandmother didn't need of clothing. She had dresses that she hadn't even worn;

however, I knew that maybe she just wanted to feel useful by sewing these dresses. On our way home, I couldn't help but wonder why God had been so good to me. I was overjoyed to be allowed to spend this wonderful time with her and see how much she enjoyed it.

My earnest wish was that I could spend more quality time with her and grandpa with whatever time they had left on earth. Ma B and I returned home. As I was seated on my bed, one thing became clear to me. My emotional problems would continue to plague me for a long time to come unless I sought out help. I needed to get help. I could no longer deal with the pain on my own. I made myself a promise to seek intervention.

CHAPTER NINETEEN

Seeking the professional help needed

The following day, I went to work more determined than ever to call my health care provider, and finally, get a referral for counseling.

When I returned from my two-day absence, the workload was tedious. Before I could even log in, Randy was already calling me. I ignored the call. Lately, he had been acting as if I was a possession, and so I decided to distance myself. However, distancing myself was also my Modus Operandi. The closer a man got to me—the more I pulled away almost as if I was programmed like this. Before I had even analyzed the situation, I was ready to run.

My heart would always run free. I tried so much to be normal, but even normalcy eluded me. Over the years, I thought I would be healed with time, but time still would not let me be. All the places I had traveled, all the freelance articles I had written, and even all the daunting love poems I had swooned over could not give me any satisfaction. I was empty.

Ever since I had seen Craig a week ago my whole being had been in overdrive. I needed to stay away from him. He had such a profound effect on me. Why did he want me back? My soul was already tormented by the breakup. My world felt like a horse and carriage—all my past baggage now felt heavier. My past demons still haunted me. I still wondered why I was raped. At times, I still blamed myself. At times, I still carried the shame, the guilt, and the aftermath. I still carried the secret. Even Ma B, who had been there for me throughout that traumatic event, was now telling me to seek professional help. When I was with Craig, all was well because I had drowned all my emotional pain in the sex with him. He was my fix—my cure. I could ignore the fact that I was only going deeper and deeper into the darkness. As I sat ruminating at my desk, I could feel tears stinging my eyes. They weren't far away.

I quickly composed myself before I had to meet my next client. The client wanted me to save his house by removing it from an auction listing. I listened to his story about why he was behind on his mortgage. He had fallen on tough times and could not keep up with the payments. He pleaded with me. He informed me he had a wife and two small kids. Where would they go? That was not my problem, but I was sympathetic to him. I remembered my own struggles. I told him that I would give him thirty days to produce at least one month's payment, and then he could go on a payment plan if he came through with the one-month payment. He left feeling a little relieved.

I always felt empathy for others. I knew all about how life could deal you a hard blow through no fault of your own. I knew how losing a job and finding another could be incredibly challenging. As I reflected on my own job struggles, I wondered about my earthly guardian angel. If she hadn't pointed me in the direction of spiritual cleansing, would I have been in the same position as my client? Where would I be? What would have happened to me? I never saw her again. I never got the chance to thank her for helping a stranger. Every time, I passed the bus stop I would always look out for her. I even used to walk with a small token of appreciation in my pocketbook if I ever ran into her again. Life always had a way of turning to the good or to the bad, and my hope had always been to be the absolute best I could be—on whatever side of the coin life was on.

The phone rang and once again it was Randy calling. I warmly greeted him and told him I couldn't do lunch. I also had to reassure him that everything was okay with me. He said he heard in the tone of my voice that something was amiss. My voice always betrayed me—no matter how hard

I tried to convince people. I quickly dismissed his worries and continued working.

I didn't know how I was going to get away from him after work, but I told myself I would cross that bridge when I got there. I looked at the time. I still had another five hours to go. I told my friend at the front desk I was expecting lunch. She just looked me up and down but did not comment. I decided to stay and do overtime, but a fight with Randy was probably brewing on the horizon. If we fought, I was going to remain reserved no matter what.

As I was leaving for the day, I realized that the day was over, and I still had not taken the first step toward seeking counseling. I sat on the toilet seat in the restroom and wept. "Oh God, help me." I felt like I was going to have a nervous breakdown. Suddenly, I composed myself. I started repeating Psalm 23 (KJV). What could have gotten over me these last couple of days?

I told Caroline that I was spending the night with her. She could get me out of this funk. Caroline was always happy and talkative. She had a great personality. We talked, laughed, and drank Stone Ginger wine. That night, I prayed a special prayer to God begging for clarity in my life.

CHAPTER TWENTY

Standing my ground

I was seated in Randy's living room looking across at Randy. He has been silent all evening. How could I get away from him?

"You are the 'Lady of the House' now," he said. I stared at him—dumbfounded by his statement. "Now, you will live here."

I stared at him for a long time then I firmly said, "No, I am not. I don't want to live here." I know I didn't live anywhere as impressive looking like this mansion with its many bedrooms and attached swimming pool, but I didn't want to be elevated to this mansion.

He pulled me close to him. "Why, babe? I thought you liked it here."

"Yes, I do, but this will never be my home."

He took two beers from the refrigerator. He handed one to me. "I want you here with me. You've traveled. You're intelligent. You're classy and just plain bright. I want you as my partner," he rambled on. "This is an offer to die for. Any woman would say yes."

"True, but I am not any woman." I continued, "I am wounded. I have deep emotional scars, and I am carrying an indelible memory."

"Whatever it is, you will be healed with time," he insisted.

We drank a couple more beers, and then he asked me to stay the night. I knew I would already be spending the night, but I also knew that I couldn't accept his prior offer. I could feel myself plunging deeper and deeper into this valley of darkness with no light in sight.

I took the next two days off from work to deal with personal business. I went to see my brother. My younger brother, Johnny, lived in Kingston with his daughter, Kayla, and her mother, Joy. He was working and trying to build a life for himself; however, it was difficult for him. He had a job, but the pay was minimal. Mom tried to help as much as she could, but it was still difficult for her when she had bills of her own. Living in any of the ghetto areas in Kingston had its challenges, and Woodpecker Avenue which ran off Waltham Park Road was no different. The high crime rate, the zinc fencing which served as a barricade, and the tenement yards were evidence of the poverty that plagued these areas. However, something loomed on the horizon.

The next morning, my brother and I had an interview at the U.S. Embassy. My mom had filed for us to get permanent U.S. residency visas. My brother, Kayla, JJ, and I all showed up for the interview while Joy and my daughter waited outside for us. The interview went well, and we were given the residency visa stamp on our passports. My brother was incredibly happy. Finally, he was getting a chance to leave the ghetto and take his daughter with him. I didn't want to leave because I wanted to keep my job for a while. I was also in the process of legally adopting my daughter. We had a few months to leave on the permanent residency visa. I hugged my brother. I was so happy for him. All six of us walked towards Oxford Road.

That evening, we sat in my brother's tiny apartment reflecting on the day's events and what this meant for us. I wasn't yet ready to live in New York like he was. In the meantime, our mom was looking for a larger place to rent so that we could move in with her. Randy seemed happy for us, but I knew he wanted me to stay with him. He kept saying, "You're now a permanent resident of the States, and one day you are going to leave me."

I woke up in the middle of the night, and Randy wasn't there beside me. I walked into the bathroom, and there he was—snorting coke. He didn't notice me. I stood there for a couple of seconds and then walked back into the bedroom. I buried my head in the pillow and wept. This was the first time I knew he was doing both weed and coke. It was then that I began to form a plan to permanently get away from him. Was I already in too deep? I couldn't sleep for the rest of the night.

The next morning, I got up early, made breakfast, and we seated ourselves at the kitchen table talking about the news coming out of New York. His satellite dish transmitted more channels than he had time to watch. I got dressed for work.

As we took the short ride to Halfway Tree Road, he asked, "Seriously, will you ever be mine?"

I smiled at him. "One day. I might." He kissed me warmly on the cheek as I alighted from the car.

That morning at work, I came to the realization that I was going to walk away from him soon. I could not pursue or maintain a relationship—with Randy or with anyone. I was just too emotionally screwed up. However, I couldn't rush our breakup. Randy was dangerous, or so I kept telling myself. But was he really all that dangerous? Or was I just trying to justify my need to plan an escape?

Later that day, I called my doctor at St. Joseph Medical Center and asked him for a referral. Did I need psychiatric help or just personal counseling? I always had adhered to the fact that if someone walked out of your life to never let them take your dreams and aspirations with them. My cousin, Buck, reinforced that belief when he sent me a similar quote. I was going to fight no matter what. I had come too far to turn back now. I would own this and bravely come to terms with it for the last time. No longer would I walk around with this burden. No longer would I have bottled up the emotions weighing me down. I would come out into my own.

My counselor was a middle-aged heavy-set woman. She introduced herself and asked me, "What bought you here?"

I thought to myself, 'This is a big mistake, and I should just leave.' But I couldn't back out. "I need help."

She looked me over and then asked, "What took you so long?"

I just stared at her with my big, brown eyes. I reached for my pocketbook and stood up. When she said, "If you can't answer the basic questions, how are you going to answer the tough ones?"

I did not move. She switched subjects. "Tell me about yourself, and your biggest accomplishment so far."

I wasn't in it for this. I thought we may have started off on the wrong note. That is how twisted up I was about counseling. This lady didn't know me and was only trying to do her job. I calmed down and began summarizing my answers. I watched as she took notes on a legal pad. My forty-five minutes were over, and I was so desperate to run out of there. I felt so uncomfortable in her presence. However, I reminded myself that I wasn't going to chicken out. I was going to keep my second appointment with Miss Ruby J.

That evening, Randy asked. "Why are you going to counseling?"

"For my past indiscretions." He just laughed and shook his head.

It was incredibly interesting to analyze my life and put my journey so far into perspective. The highs and the lows, the pains and the gains, the doubts and the bouts of confidence, the weaknesses, and the strengths. In the end, it felt like a paradise gained, then ultimately, a paradise lost.

CHAPTER TWENTY-ONE

Laying it all out

I sat in Miss Ruby J's office. I noticed for the first time the mountain of papers haphazardly scattered all over her desk. My goodness! How could she function like this? The plant that stood in the corner of her office had dried, withered leaves. It badly needed watering. I moved my eyes toward her as she peeped over her reading glasses to look at me. I shook my head in disgust.

"We will begin where we left off the last time," she stated.

I composed myself for her questions, despite feeling drained of all emotion. Suddenly, the phone on her desk rang. She reached for the receiver looking annoyed. I just rolled my eyes at the situation. She curtly answered the person, hung up the phone, and stormed out the office door. Could this get any worse? I stood up and walked towards the wall on which her certifications hung and read each one aloud as if talking to myself. She hastily walked back in. "Let's begin, shall we?"

"How did your mother leaving you made you feel?" I blurted out the answer I had already rehearsed in anticipating this question. "You lack candor," she said.

"I lack many things."

If she was surprised at my counterstatement, her demeanor betrayed nothing. "You're not at war with me."

I pretended not to hear her. This wasn't going well, and I didn't plan on wasting my forty-five minutes going back and forth with her. I crossed my legs, dangled my six-inch heels, and tried to get comfortable so that my nerves could stay in check.

Miss Ruby J shuffled through her notes like a rough deck of cards and finally asked her next question. "In retrospect, what are the things you blame yourself for?"

"Being born."

She wasn't expecting that answer, but replied, "You should be grateful."

Both of us remained silent for a while, and then she asked, "Would you like to have another counselor?"

"No," I flatly stated. I thought to myself, 'I'm not going to start all over again from the beginning.'

"You have to be mindful that my job is not to judge you, and whatever you are revealing to me stays in confidence. My job is to help you through this process by being your mediator." She said trying to reassure me.

I left her office. "I'm not going back—to hell with it."

As I looked at my sleeping kids that night, I knew that I had to do whatever it took to make me whole. I stayed up most of the night wrestling with myself. People have said that the darkest hour is just before dawn, but my thoughts were taking me to a place so dark and deep that I couldn't believe dawn was coming. My voice cried out in the silence of the moment, and I fell to the floor in anguish.

I must have dozed off though because I was awoken by the crowing of a roaster in the backyard. At night, all the fowls slept in the ackee tree. I picked myself up off the floor and went to the kitchen to put the kettle on. Before the kettle screamed, I went to retrieve my Bible from the nightstand. I sat at the kitchen table with a cup of coffee. As Ma B made her way to join me, I made her a cup of tea.

I opened the bible to Psalm 91 (KJV) and read it aloud. As a child, I remember Ma B would always recite the words of this Psalm, and during my most trying times I had come to rely on this Psalm for comfort. Ma B and I started praying together. When we were done, I felt the presence of

God moving in my heart. I remembered the story of Paul and Silas praying together. It was always my belief that if either one of them had prayed alone then nothing would have happened. That is why when both came together under one accord, they were able to get the prison doors opened. I felt that my grandmother praying with me could give me the desired results I was looking for. Ma B had been encouraging me to rededicate my life to God. She had been pushing me toward consecration for a while. However, that was something I had to do on my own. I was getting closer to the realization that something would have to give.

I arrived at work early and felt good in my spirit. I felt at peace. My soul was about to speak to my intellectual mind and bring forth a precise decision that would place my life on a different path. Why could things never stay the same for me? Why was I always caught up in some emotional battle?

It was a new day, and I had adhered to its possibilities. Anything and everything were about to change. I told Randy that I would be spending the night with Caroline. He just said, "Okay," and let me be. It was her birthday after all. We planned to go to a club after work to hang out and enjoy ourselves. But instead, we scrapped that plan and decided to go to dinner. I felt guilty about going to clubs while I was inclined to follow Jesus. The restaurant was superb, and the waitress was courteous and friendly. The candles on each table reflected a warm and welcoming atmosphere. We ordered a bottle of red wine.

As the waitress poured from the bottle, it dawned on me how close we had become. On the first day on the job, I felt an instant likeness towards her. She dressed well and demonstrated a good command of the computer terminal when she retrieved customers' information. I watched Caroline's work ethic and was impressed. She was very easy to talk to and offered to guide me through the learning process. I marveled at the level of complexity the job entailed and was grateful for her assistance. Caroline was my new best friend. As weeks passed, I realized that Caroline, my sister from another mother, was the real deal. She was genuine. I raised my glass to her. We had come a long way together, and through it all, she had been my confidant, my sister, and my friend. As we finished our dinner and drinks, a young man walked over to us and said, "Happy birthday." She smiled, and said, "Thank you." It was almost 9:00 p.m. when we left. All was good. God had blessed us tremendously, and to him, we gave our praises.

CHAPTER TWENTY-TWO

Coming out at last

The sun lazily rose over the mountains, and from where I was standing the warm glow came cracking through the window glass. Oh, how I loved both the rising and the setting of the sun.

Today, I was about to have the most intense session with Miss Ruby J.

Last night, I prayed for strength. I prayed for courage. I prayed for wisdom. This was the time when the fowls all came home to roost.

I dressed in my uniform and choose a yellow scarf with matching yellow heels. I decided to wear my two gold bracelets. I adjusted the rings on my fingers. I checked to make sure my earrings were locked in. As I looked over myself in the mirror, I made sure to look myself in the eyes. For the first time, in a long time, I was able to smile back at myself. I touched the crucifix attached to the necklace on my chest and made the sign of the cross. I loved the transformation I witnessed in myself. Yes, I had blossomed into my own woman. I picked up my pocketbook and headed for the door.

Miss Ruby J was surprised to see me looking so vibrant. "You're early, and you look like a new woman," she greeted.

I smiled at her. I took my usual seat while she fumbled through papers on her desk. Each time I went to her office, I still wondered how she could possibly manage to function among all the clutter. The plant was coming back to life as she started watering it again. I turned my attention toward her again and watched her with an amused expression.

"Let's begin," she flatly stated. "Today, we will talk about your molestation and the aftermath," she stated in a serious tone.

I looked at her. I meet her eyes. I was ready to get this over with.

She continued, "Tell me from the beginning. How did you come to know him? And what led up to the encounter that night?"

I deeply inhaled. I gathered my thoughts and began my story. Not once, did she interrupt me or ask a follow-up question. I told her everything. When I finally stopped talking, she said, "You never cease to amaze me."

"Next session, we will talk about "letting go."

I left her office and headed to work. I was so proud of myself for not breaking down in tears. I think it even surprised her too. I sat at my desk, drinking my favorite cup of coffee, and a great relief flood me. I was going to free myself of this burden I had been carrying all these years. I was no longer going to feel guilty. I was done with thinking it was my fault. Today was a good day. It was the day to begin letting go of these demons that had tormented me over the years.

I called Randy. "Can we do lunch?"

If he was surprised, he didn't let on. "Sure, anything for you."

I smiled to myself. I knew he harbored deep feelings for me, but I did not know whether he really loved me or not. I couldn't measure his love based on material or monetary gifts. I knew he carried secrets too. I knew he was in a dark place. And I also knew that I couldn't get him to kick his habits. My fear of being with him overruled my better judgment of the life I could have shared with him. Were we two lost souls bought together by fate?

I had a meeting then it was going to be my lunchtime. I hadn't felt so happy and bold in a long time. I received more good news as well. My boss had just given me a merit raise. All my hard work was paying off.

Randy took me to his favorite Chinese restaurant on Red Hills Road. As we dined, he asked, "How is your therapy going?"

"Great!" I happily replied.

"You look great." He continued, "You want to tell me now why the therapy?"

"I told you already."

He put his hands on mine. "I am proud of you. I like your new attitude. Whatever it is, you are working through it, and that's a good thing." I looked up as he continued, "Do I have to wait until you fix everything in your life before you consider ours?"

"No, I won't let you wait, but I have to fix me."

With that, we completed our meals and headed back to work. I told him about my raise, and he was delighted.

That evening, I worked overtime and waited for my ride. Tonight, belonged to Ma B. I could finally tell her I had cleansed myself from the past, and that I was so grateful to her for being there for me. I told Randy I needed to go home, so he took the long ride through the Junction Road and dropped me off. My cousin Paul and Randy always burned ganja spiffs together, and tonight was no different. I walked towards the beach house where he had parked and watched as they rolled the weed into the paper and lit up. This was going to be a long night. Randy ordered beer for himself and my cousin. Then, for all the other fellows on the corner that came over to smoke with them. He told them to order whatever they wanted.

I wasn't going to hang out with them, so I slowly walked away to share the good news with Ma B. She hugged me so tight. I could hardly breathe. When she finally let me go, there were streaks of tears rolling down her cheeks. I gently wiped them away. We sat in the kitchen, drank Peppermint tea, and reminisced on all the times I had vowed to seek counseling, but couldn't bring myself to do it. I was ashamed of my dirty laundry being exposed. I was terrified that my friends would know the secret and harshly judge me. I was so mixed up in my head. Even though I knew it was the right thing to do, I convinced myself that it wasn't for me.

Craig and his notion of 'wanting to get back with me,' and the emotional destruction which threatened me had forced me into action. Being in Craig's very presence was too much for me to handle, and the wave of emotions that followed had brought me to the brink of despair once more. Now, I was different. I looked at Ma B. I knew how much she loved me, and how much she too had carried this burden. I hugged her. Finally, I felt free. That night seemed silent except for the laughter coming from the beach house. The Laughter of free spirits and unburdened minds. The Laughter of the present, and the Laughter of the living

CHAPTER TWENTY-THREE

The one I love ♥ the most

I took a week off from work to spend quality time with Ma B, Grandpa P, and the kids. Ma B was getting older, and so was Grandpa P. I thought she needed a well-deserved break from the house chores, so I decided to help her

Taking care of Grandpa had become a full-time job. He was getting older and couldn't look after himself anymore. The old man was also getting more stubborn and grumpy. On that day, he didn't want a sponge bath. He didn't want me to touch his body. I tried to calm him down by reading him his favorite scripture, Psalm 91 (KJV). After putting him in clean clothes and feeding him his oatmeal, I took him outside to sit in the backyard, enjoy the warm sunlight, and gentle breeze.

The kids were already at school, so Ma B and I settled down to do the laundry. I could see this was getting too much for her. Ma B had agreed to let me hire Miss Clare, a lady who worked in the area, to wash and dry the laundry. Miss Clare would come two days per week because of the number of bed linens being used up. Miss Clare was to start her job on Friday and going forward she would come on Tuesdays and Fridays. With that settled, I moved on to the other house chores at hand.

After the first two days, I had pretty much taken care of all the things pertaining to the smooth running of the house. Miss Lana was going to help with getting Grandpa up in the mornings from now on. Even though she never complained, I could see how much of a relief that was for Ma B.

It was a warm and beautiful Thursday morning. The sun was rising against the clouds over the hills, and the dashing waves were crashing on the shores as we waited for our ride into Kingston. Today was very special for me, and I was very upbeat. Today, Ma B and Miss Ruby J would finally meet each other. This came about when I told Miss Ruby J that I would love to have Ma B sit in on the "Letting Go" session. At first, she refused. She didn't want any distractions, but I was able to persuade her that this could ultimately work in my favor.

As Ma B and I sat in the waiting area, I reflected on how far we had come together as mother and daughter because she was indeed my mother. My eyes became watery. Where would I be without this kind soul? When my grandfather and my paternal grandmother parted ways, my grandfather met Ma B and realized she was the one. They soon moved in together. Ma B worked at the Great House on Pringle Hill in St. Mary Parish and was loved by everyone.

My mother went to England to seek a better life. By then, she had birthed three children—my twin brother and I, and my baby brother. She left me with Grandpa P and Ma B, and my two brothers with her mom. Ma B was delighted to have me. She had birthed two boys, who died at an early age, so I became her world. Even with all my childhood illnesses, she nurtured me, unconditionally loved me, and never gave up on me. Even now, as I was about to put this ugly episode behind me, she was right there supporting me. She must have read my thoughts as she squeezed my hand in hers. I looked up at her, and she gave me that familiar wink that reassured me everything was going to be all right.

Miss Ruby J was now ready to see me, and so we entered her office. I immediately noticed the changes. For once, her desk was clean and tidy. The files were neatly stacked on her table instead of scrambled everywhere. The flowers and plants now showed signs of life and looked like they were freshly watered. An air of cleanliness filled the room and for the first time, I felt like I could freely breathe.

I sat in my usual seat, and Ma B occupied the seat beside me holding and rubbing my hand.

"This is my grandmother and Second Mother, Ma B," I said as I introduced her.

"Nice to meet you, Ma B," Miss Ruby J said.

"Same here," Ma B replied.

Miss Ruby J wasted no time as she addressed me. "Well, today is the day you'll let go, and walk out of here a new, free woman."

"I am looking forward to just that."

"This office was done for you. I wanted you to see the transformation." She continued, "Take a moment to look around."

I cleared my throat as I looked the room over again.

"This room represents you." She continued, "Your life was a mess just like this office was, and now it's all clean and shows a healthy work environment."

For the first time since I started with her, I wanted to cry. Ma B squeezed my hand as I regained my composure.

"Today, you graduate. And I don't want to ever see you in this building again. You are an extraordinarily strong and remarkable person. I've never had anyone like you before."

Now, I felt a teardrop and wiped it away. I looked up at Miss Ruby J, and for the first time, I saw a woman of compassion and empathy. Nowhere in our previous sessions had she shown any signs of even being human or sympathetic to my pain.

She continued, "Today, you will forgive yourself and let go of past demons. You will be free. Free from all the emotional pain, free from the unforgiving baggage, free from past indiscretions, free from the sadness and unnecessary tears, free from sleepless nights, and free from unrequited love. You mustn't guard your heart. You must let your heart run free! In so doing, you will find yourself. You will find your worth, and you will start to love yourself again. I don't usually do this, but I would like to give you a hug. May I?"

I got up, and she wrapped her big, strong arms around me. For that brief moment, I felt safe.

I thanked her for listening to me without judging me. I thanked her for tolerating my antics, and at times pushing through my rudeness.

She hugged Ma B, and said, "You did an excellent job in raising her."

"Thank you," Ma B replied.

As we left, Miss Ruby J called out after me, "Don't come back."

Randy was waiting outside for us. I was so happy that this was finally over, and I could move on with my life, but I also knew that to move on I had to cut all the people from my past who would hinder my spiritual growth. And this meant finally leaving this man.

We stopped in the mall at Constant Spring Road and got pastries for the kids. We pulled up at his house, and Ma B was surprised to see how huge it really was. He took her on a tour while I helped Miss Maud fix lunch for us. Ma B came to the table after she had toured the house and looked me straight in the eyes as she asked, "Why did you say no? This could be good for the kids." I sat in silence. I could tell that no sooner had those words left her mouth than she regretted them.

At the table, we made small talk. Miss Maud joined us like she always did when I was around. I always treated her as one of the family and not as the hired help. We chatted light-heartedly, and I helped her clear the table and do the dishes. In the early evening, we sat by the poolside having drinks. Ma B was delighted to see how we were all getting along. As the evening clouds gathered across the sky with the setting sun, a beautiful rainbow flowed out of the sky like a sign of Hope.

Randy was getting ready to take us home. I could tell Ma B was having a good time. She and Miss Maud were chatting and laughing. As I got my pocketbook, Randy came up beside me.

"Ma B thinks you should live here with me."

"Really?"

"Yes, everyone can't be wrong," he defiantly said.

"Time will tell."

Ma B bade Miss Maud goodbye and walked towards the car.

I sat in the back while Ma B rode upfront with Randy. I felt so good. I smiled as I remembered Miss Ruby J's parting words. I immersed myself in these counseling sessions. I had given it my all, and now I felt so liberated.

The next week, I returned to work feeling on top of the world. I ordered a nice fruit basket and sent it to Miss Ruby

J's office anonymously. I was surprised when my phone rang and the lady at the other end said.

"I am calling on behalf of Miss Ruby J. She said, 'Thank you.'"

"For what?"

"The lovely fruit basket."

She knew it was from me. Well, so much for wanting to be anonymous.

I focused on the mortgage account in front of me wondering if I could help save someone's house. I looked over the list a second time and walked into my manager's office. He looked up from the report he was reading as I pulled the chair closer to his desk. I handed him the list. We both diligently worked to see who we could save from losing their house at an upcoming auction. We were able to eliminate five customers from the list. I loved my job. At the end of the day, it felt so rewarding.

My friend, Faithy, was getting ready to go to London for a vacation. I was so happy for her. I was going to miss her tremendously. My sweet cousin, Sherri, wanted to go to New York for two weeks. My mom had told her that she could stay with her, but that she wasn't going to have the time to show her around the city. I eagerly volunteered to

go with her—not knowing that this hastily made decision
was going to impact the rest of my life.

CHAPTER TWENTY-FOUR

Escaping from myself

I found myself pulling away from the relationship with Randy. He kept asking me what was wrong, but I always remained silent.

One evening, I was in the kitchen with Miss Maud while he was on the phone shouting at the person on the other end. I was taken aback by the volume of his tone.

"Brenda wants to come home," Miss Maud said.

"Really?" I asked.

I whispered a silent prayer of thanks to God. This could be the answer to my prayers. Brenda was the 'Lady of the House,' and went by his last name. She also told everyone that she was his wife. She was from Costa Rica. They met in New York during their Kingpin days. After they left the States, they moved back to Jamaica together.

The first time I met her she told me, "My husband is fixed on you."

"So true," I replied as she walked away.

Then, she had left for Costa Rica, and vowed never to return.

Later that evening, on my way home, Randy told me about Brenda and her wanting to come home. I listened to him, and then choose my next words wisely.

"When is she coming?"

"Next week."

I turned my face towards the window, and a shy smile crept over my lips. "Your wife is coming home. You should be happy," I sarcastically stated.

"Brenda is not my wife. I am not married. She goes around saying she is my wife because of the neighborhood we live in."

I said nothing. I saw her coming home as the answer to my prayers. Later that night, he assured me nothing was going to change between us. My heart just sunk. How could this be? It rang true to the saying, "The more things change, the more things remain the same."

But in this situation, something had to give. I needed to get away from him so badly, and for the first time ever I was definitely afraid of leaving him. This wasn't a man you just walked away from without getting permission to do so. Even though I hadn't seen him exhibit any sign of violence, my instincts told me I was treading on troubled waters. What had I gotten myself into?

Now, I was really looking forward to my two weeks' reprieve in New York City—the Big Apple. The city that never sleeps. We were leaving in two days, and those two days couldn't come fast enough. I was so excited to be going on this trip. After I had completed my counseling sessions, a new wave of clarity washed over me, and now I could see clearly.

I went grocery shopping for Ma B and left her money to keep the house running and for any emergency. As I was talking to her and telling her to take care of the kids, she put my hands to her heart and asked, "Why am I so fearful that you're not coming back?" I pulled away from her. "Please don't say that."

I looked at my grandfather—old and frail—lying in bed with his bible. I asked him to sing his favorite song for me. As he began to sing that glorious song, "Draw Me Nearer," my eyes became wet with tears. I sat on the bed with him. I told him how much I loved him and how grateful I was that he raised me. Then, out of nowhere, he asked, "Were you ever raped?" The question took me by surprise, but I calmly said, "Yes, but that was a long time ago. I am over it now." He looked at me and nodded his head in agreement with me. I found the whole thing very strange. Why was he asking me now if he had suspected it all along? I placed my lips on his forehead and rubbed my hands across his chest. Somehow, this encounter seemed so different. Back then, what I didn't know was that this was the last time I would see my dear grandfather alive.

We arrived in New York and took a cab to my mom's new address. The flight was on time. And despite me handing the Immigration officer my large package from the embassy in Kingston, my process time was minimal. Now, I was officially a Permanent Resident of the United States, and it felt really good.

My mom and sister were delighted to have us. My mom went to bed early while my cousin, sister, and I stayed up watching movies. The next day, we rode the train into Manhattan. We got off at 34th Street and 7th Avenue and hit up the Macy's department store. I wasn't buying any merchandise to take back with me to the job this time. I was only buying for my family. We hit all the stores in the vicinity that day. We went to Madison Square Garden and then took the subway back home.

At home, we were seated in the living room watching the news and conversing about the bible. My mother was on her way to being a Missionary. She was saved and baptized but was not fulfilled. I remember her fasting, praying, and waiting to get "the Gift of speaking in tongues." My mom's journey took me back to Acts chapter 2 (KJV) which teaches about the day of Pentecost and of speaking in tongues. I had learned from the bible that speaking in tongues was never meant for man to understand. It was a direct line from God. My sister was surprised to know I was so educated on the bible.

CHAPTER TWENTY-FIVE

The only way out

I woke up early and saw my mom off to work. My sister was hanging out with us that day, even though she was more interested in spending time with my cousin. They were closer in age, and so maybe she could relate to her better.

After breakfast, we were traveling to Rockefeller Center in Manhattan. Suddenly, I wanted to stay home so I did. I called Randy to see how he was doing. Brenda answered the phone instead. I told her I was calling to speak with Randy. She just hung up the phone. I lay down in the living room and tried to sleep, but I couldn't. I passed the time watching the "Sally Jessy Raphael" show. After the show, I tried calling Caroline. We talked for about ten minutes. I really missed her and all my coworkers. Later, I planned a trip to Atlantic City. My cousin was delighted. The next day, we went to Atlantic City. We spent the night. It was so much fun.

We arrived back home and stopped in Manhattan. We went to the store all foreigners visit—Century 21. Shoes,

Shoes, Shoes. We bought them all! It was so much fun shopping in that store. Wow! We got home, packed our stuff, and headed for the Prayer Meeting at my mom's church. It was divine.

The next day, we relaxed in the morning and went to Orchard Beach in the Bronx. All was well. I took time on this trip to see myself for the first time as a free spirit. I couldn't have been happier. I basked in my newfound glow of redemption and took time out to give God thanks for his goodness and mercy. It was fitting to say, "I was drinking from my saucer because my cup was overflowing."

The second week of our vacation rolled around, and we were trying to find activities to do. My sister had returned to work, so it was just my cousin and I doing some last-minute shopping. As our vacation came to an end, the reality of going back home began to formulate in my thoughts. It suddenly dawned on me that my problem back home with Randy was far from over. I had spoken to him the night before and let him know that I wanted out of the relationship. He listened but didn't say much. I couldn't read whether he was okay with the breakup or refusing to accept it. I took him as not giving me a definite response as the latter.

My thinking went into overdrive as I pondered the circumstance trying to find a solution. During my vacation, I had put this lingering situation on the back burner, but now it was at the forefront. This was the only situation where I had no concrete solution, and it could turn out to be the most dangerous one. Was this all in my head? Was I overreacting? The thought of my body washing up on a seashore in Jamaica or being found somewhere riddled with bullets frightened me into action. For the first time since my sessions were over, I was very afraid. I thought about all the unfinished business I had to take care of. I thought of my kids. I thought of Ma B and Grandpa P, who had given me their all. I thought of being taken away from them entirely. Suddenly, I knew the answer to my predicament.

The day before we were to arrive home, I had a private conversation with my mom. I was hoping she would keep it confidential. I had a similar one with my cousin. It was final.

That night, Randy had called to confirm the arrival of our flight to Jamaica. The following afternoon, all was well. We had finished packing and decided to go for a walk around the block. My cousin had tried to see if we could change our course and abort the plan for a while, but time was not on my hands. On the ride to JFK, my heart was pounding. I kept thinking, 'What have you done?' I pushed back my tears and braced myself. Was it too late? Yes, it was too late for me. I couldn't turn back the hands of time. All I could do now was shallow this bitter pill. This was the only way.

The placid look on my cousin's face said it all. I had drawn all of them into a tangled web. In retrospect, I should've shunned away from Randy in the beginning, but even with all my craziness and indiscretions I never would have thought that it would have come down to this finale. Ma B said, "In every bad situation, give thanks because it always could have been worse." Was my worst yet to come or was I just being paranoid? I didn't have more time to think. We arrived at the airport and checked in all our bags. We paid the fees for the extra luggage and waited. A dark cloud blanketed over me, and I shuddered.

My cousin gave me one last hug and walked towards the checkpoint. I knew I wasn't being fair to her. I thought about all the responsibilities I had just laid on her. But we were family. Even though she was thirteen years younger than me, we were very close, and so I knew I could count on her. She might have felt obligated to accommodate my madness or pity over my plight.

I listened to the boarding announcement for the flight. I listened as my name rang over the intercom three times,

"Last call for Verona Mitchell." Then, I turned and slowly walked towards the taxi stand.

THE END

www.ingramcontent.com/pod-product-compliance
Lightning Source LLC
Chambersburg PA
CBHW060133100426
42744CB00007B/774